The

Wiccan Spell Manual

The
Wiccan Spell Manual

Sirona Knight

CITADEL PRESS
Kensington Publishing Corp.
www.kensingtonbooks.com

CITADEL PRESS books are published by

Kensington Publishing Corp.
850 Third Avenue
New York, NY 10022

Copyright © 2001 Sirona Knight

All Kensington titles, imprints, and distributed lines are available at special quantity discounts for bulk purchases for sales promotions, premiums, fund-raising, educational, or institutional use. Special book excerpts or customized printings can also be created to fit specific needs. For details, write or phone the office of the Kensington special sales manager: Kensington Publishing Corp., 850 Third Avenue, New York, NY 10022, attn: Special Sales Department, phone 1-800-221-2647.

Citadel Press and the Citadel logo are trademarks of Kensington Publishing Corp.

First printing September 2001

10 9 8 7 6 5 4 3 2 1

Printed in the United States of America

Cataloging data for this title may be obtained from the Library of Congress.

ISBN 0-8065-2357-3

For Sky and Michael,
And the magick they bring into my life.

ACKNOWLEDGMENTS

I would like to especially thank and acknowledge Bruce Bender for his continued faith in my writing. Many heartfelt thanks to Margaret Wolf and Renata Butera for their excellent editing skills, kindness, and continued patience. Special thanks and appreciation to Steven Zacharius, my publisher, for kindling the magickal spirit by publishing this kit. Loving blessings to my agent, Lisa Hagan, for her friendship and enthusiasm. And I would like to thank everyone who uses this kit to make positive magick.

Loving thanks, hugs, and watermelon kisses to my family and friends. Respectful thanks, to the goddesses and gods, to my ancestors, and the sacred land. I would also like to thank the extraordinary witches in my life, including Patricia Telesco, Dorothy Morrison, A. J. Drew, Skye Alexander, Raven Grimassi, Phyllis Currot, Raymond

Buckland, Gerina Dunwich, Lady Sabrina, Z. Budapest, Starhawk, Marion Weinstein, and Silver RavenWolf. Thank you all for sharing your magick and making the world brighter!

CONTENTS

INTRODUCTION

Merry Meet!

Have you ever wanted to cast a magick spell but didn't know how? Or do you know someone who would like to learn to cast magick spells? If your answer is yes to either question, this spell kit is perfectly suited to fulfill your needs. It provides step-by-step instructions plus the items you'll need to successfully practice magick. With over forty spells formulated to enrich daily life in the twenty-first century, you can use this kit to sweep magick right out of the broom closet and into your home.

Lately everyone I talk with wants to learn more about magick, how to commune with the Goddess and God, and how to cast spells to get the desired results and live the kind of life they have always imagined. There are a multitude of reasons for this. Many of us are connecting to the Pagan roots of our European ancestry, such as Celtic, Roman, and Greek, while others are looking for a spiritual practice that better matches (and recognizes) their hopes, ethics, and lifestyle. Still others are interested in magick because of popular culture and literature. For example, the enormously successful *Harry Potter* books have propelled magick into the awareness of mainstream audiences.

A renewed interest in positive magick and spell casting is creating new generations of witches called Wiccans. Wicca is a spirituality that attracts independent forward-thinkers and welcomes those individuals who have profound faith in personal freedom. It is a spiritual path for people who dare to follow their visions and dreams, for those who hear a different drummer—one that beats in step with Mother Earth's heartbeat.

This book and kit do not adhere to any specific Wiccan tradition or path, but cover the basic beliefs and practices most of us have in common. It is not intended to be a "witch in a box." Just opening the box, reading this book, using the items included, and casting the spells will not make you a Wiccan witch. Remember, the Craft is a way of life, not a fashion statement. It's not about blindly believing in the power of candle wax and magick wands.

Most Wiccans go through a basic initiation process before becoming a full-fledged witch. The initiation can be a self-dedication, or you can get initiated by an existing Wiccan group or coven. Today you can even do your initiation on the Internet! The important thing is to go through some kind of initiation, because it is a process in which you are reborn—a time of casting off your old self and becoming your new self.

There are many excellent books written by practicing Wicca authors that discuss self-dedications and initiations; please refer to the Suggested Reading list for specific titles. I encourage you to do either a self-dedication or initiation from one of these books. It is also possible to locate an active coven with people and practices that you like, and ask to be initiated by their High Priest and High Priestess. You can use the Internet and Wiccan resource books to find local groups.

Making magick requires that you have a clear intent and a focused mind: The clearer your intent and the more focused your mind, the more powerful your magick will be. The real key in making magick is communing with the divine, the Goddess and God, tapping into that divine energy, and then directing it toward a specific goal. The whole concept of this kit is to help you develop your natural talents and divine abilities. I assure you that once you dive into magick making, you will find the water is fine!

Whether just curious, a novice witch, or a practicing Wiccan, you will find this valuable kit and accompanying book will be useful and informative. Chapter One explores modern Wicca, its traditions, practices, and ethics. It explains the faces of the Goddess and God, plus the three steps of magick: expectation, desire, and merging. Chapter Two describes the best times of the day, week, and year to spin spells, as well as lunar Esbats and solar Sabbats. Chapter Three teaches about the magickal focals of the Craft as well as essential information on the elements, color, and words of power that can be used in the Craft. Chapter Four shows how to create sacred space, set up an altar, gather your magick tools, and draw the magick circle. Chapter Five lists magick spells for enhancing your daily life.

The items of enchantment in this kit—lavender oil, sage smudging wand, pentacle, tumbled quartz crystal, and miniature broom—are integrated into the spells in this book. You can do many of the spells in Chapter Five simply with these items, and you can easily do any of the other spells by adding a few candles and gathering together easy-to-find household items. With practice and repetition, you will soon discover that the spells you cast will come to fruition almost immediately after you perform them. Others may take a little longer, so be patient and keep casting.

All of the spells in this manual can be used to address everyday concerns such as love, health, prosperity, protection, and empowerment. These spells can help increase your personal energy, smooth your path, and generally help you attain wished-for results.

The spells are formulated with positive intention, and directed toward a specific expectation that is for "the good of all and the harm of none." This is definitely a "Glenda the Good Witch" kind of kit, with nothing Satanic or evil about it. So, if you want to turn your boyfriend into a toad, look elsewhere, but if you really want to make your dreams come true, then read this book, and spin the spells within its pages.

At the end of each chapter there are also some blank pages so you can make notes of gods and goddesses you'd like to work with, note special times for spells or particular Esbats and Sabbats, list focals you have or need, sketch ideas for altar set-ups, and keep track of favorites spells or variations of spells that you've tried from this spell kit. Use these pages in whatever way you find helpful, and use the whole book as a guide along the journey of the Craft.

I encourage each one of you who use this kit and read this book to make magick an everyday practice. Be bold and seek out the magick. Discover new spiritual frontiers as you enrich your life, and remember to share your magick with your family, children, friends, co-workers, and pets. We are all part of a divine magickal revolution, one that can help us make our dreams

come true and live more harmoniously with
Mother Earth, ourselves, and each other.

   Merry Meet and Merry Part Again! May the
Goddess and God protect, guide, and bless you,
always. So be it! Blessed Be!

CHAPTER ONE

Modern Wicca

People who practice magick, witchcraft, or "the Craft," are called Wiccans. We are the so-called modern-day witches and wizards. Wiccan magick is like the magic in J. K. Rowling's *Harry Potter* books, with one major distinction: Wiccan magick is fact, not fiction.

Magick is an art and a craft that has been passed down since the dawn of humanity. In "The Witches' Creed," Doreen Valiente writes:

> The power was passed down the ages,
> Each time between woman and man
> Each century unto the other,
> Ere times and the ages began.

The word "magick" actually stems from the word "Magi," the name for Persian priests who were the first astronomers and healers. Wiccan magick celebrates life. The modern renewal of nature-oriented, Earth-spirited practices, Wicca stems from the pre-Christian Pagan practices called the Old Religion, which were greatly influenced by the Druids. Over the past three thousand years, these European shamanic practices, called the Mystery Traditions, have been kept (sometimes secretly) for everyone.

Now more than ever, Wicca is relevant and applicable for people of all walks of life. The beauty of Wicca is that it's open to everyone, and everyone can benefit from its practices. An oral tradition passed from one generation to the next, Wicca honors and works with nature and with the goddesses and gods. It is about creativity, divine rapport, and ancestral power, not about Satan or the devil.

Reincarnation and rebirth, with the soul passing through many lives and being reborn, are two of the cornerstones of Wicca. References to this appear in "The Witches' Creed": "immortal and ever-renewing."

The practice of Wicca gives you a formula for spiritual development. A participatory revelation that can lead to a more enriching life, Wicca provides a framework for self-discovery, personal change, and empowerment. Through myth, ritual, spell crafting, poetry, music, love making, magick making, and working in harmony with the sacred Earth, Wiccans tap into the divine within and awaken the magick in every moment.

Wiccan Traditions

So you want to be a witch. You probably wonder what kind of witch you should be. The way to discover the answer is to do a little reading (refer to the Selected Readings for a list of books). You will probably want to try a few different kinds of Wicca before deciding. Many of us are eclectic Wiccans, blending different spiritual traditions together into one. For example, my form of Wicca is a blend of Welsh Druidism, the Faery tradition, Celtic Wicca, Strega, plus a little of the Norse tradition mixed with shamanism.

Many Wiccans follow their ancestral roots. Other Wiccans focus on one specific tradition. Either way, the essential aspect of Wicca is connecting with the divine within yourself and with the Goddess and God.

Contemporary Wicca owes much to Charles Leland (Aradia), Gerald Gardner, Aleister Crowley, Doreen Valiente, Alex Sanders, Eliphas Levi, Dion Fortune, S. L. MacGregor Mathers, Dr. W. Wynn Westcott, A. E. Waite, Paul Foster Case, and Israel Regardie, among others. Wicca has evolved from the more restrictive attitudes of its founders to a more open and eclectic feel, with more dos than don'ts.

There are hundreds of different traditions that come under the umbrella of "Wicca" in the United States and across the globe. Most are very tolerant of different viewpoints and lifestyles. Women and men are considered equal and there is no hierarchal doctrine. I grew up Catholic, so this idea really appealed to me! Also, there are many different Wiccan ideals and styles of worship. If you can't find one you like, you can create your own!

All Wiccans are dedicated to the responsible stewardship and protection of the Earth and to the positive evolution of consciousness. A popular religion that focuses on reuniting humanity with itself and nature, Wicca can help people reclaim their personal power.

Wicca as a religion is similar to the United States as a country in that it's a melting pot. In the case of Wicca, it is one of nature-based spiritualities, such as hedge witchcraft, Gardnerian, Faery Wicca, Dianic Wicca, Shamanic Wicca, Druidism, Strega, and so forth. This is probably one of the reasons Wicca is so popular and growing strong in America. For more information about the many Wiccan traditions, refer to my book, *Celtic Traditions* (Citadel Press, 2000).

Ethical Magick

Wiccans adhere to the last eight words of the "Wiccan Rede": "An harm ye none, do what ye will." For me, this means each of us needs to do what we love, find our calling in life, and fulfill our dreams in a way that will benefit both ourselves and others. By finding your calling, your true nature, you also connect with your divine nature within. You are the Goddess! You are the God! You are divine!

Magick can help you in your quest to discover your calling. By creating specific magickal goals, you can move your life in the direction you truly desire. A positive intention and strong desire for change are essential in successful spell crafting.

No special rules of conduct apply as Wicca is generally devoid of dogma, something that sets it apart from most other religions. The steadfast rule in spell crafting is to manipulate and direct energies toward a particular goal or purpose, but *not to manipulate people.*

It's important not to engage in negative magick. You can almost always find ways to do effective protection spells for yourself and those you love without inflicting physical, mental, or spiritual (psychic) harm. Wiccans learn how to deflect harm without causing harm by neutralizing negative energies.

Wiccans actively and intelligently defend themselves when attacked by others. We do not accept abuse or mistreatment from others, and we do not ignore darkness and evil with the hope that it will go away. Instead, we act within our spiritual center by spinning beneficial spells and following the divine voices of the goddesses, gods, our ancestors, and the sacred Earth.

The Wiccan Rede (Modern Version)

Bide ye Wiccan laws you must,
in perfect love and perfect trust.
Live ye must and let to live,
fairly take and fairly give.

For the circle thrice about
to keep unwelcome spirits out.
To bind ye spell well every time,
let the spell be spake in rhyme.

Soft of eye and light of touch,
speak ye little, listen much.
Deosil go by the waxing moon,
chanting out ye baleful tune.

When ye Lady's moon is new,
kiss ye hand to her times two.
When ye moon rides at her peak,
then ye heart's desire seek.

Heed the North winds mighty gale,
lock the door and trim the sail.
When the wind comes from the South,
Love will kiss thee on the mouth.

When the wind blows from the East,
expect the new and set the feast.
Nine woods in the cauldron go,
burn them fast and burn them slow.

Elder be ye Lady's tree,
burn it not, or cursed ye'll be.

When the wheel begins to turn,
soon ye Beltane fires will burn.

When the wheel hath turned a Yule,
light the log the Horned One rules.
Heed ye flower, bush and tree,
    by the Lady blessed be.

Where the rippling waters go,
cast a stone, the truth ye'll know.
When ye have and hold a need,
    harken not to others greed.

With a fool no season spend,
or be counted as his friend.
Merry meet and merry part,
bright the cheeks and warm the heart.

Mind ye threefold law ye should,
three times bad and three times good.
When misfortune is enow,
wear the star upon thy brow.

True in love may ye ever be,
lest thy love be false to thee.
These eight words the Wiccan Rede fulfill;
An harm ye none, do what ye will.

Magickal Power

There are four kinds of magickal power:

1. *Cosmic Power* The power of the universe, the stars, planets, comets, alien beings, nebulas, and black holes.

2. *Earth Power* The natural power of our planet and its resources.

3. *Personal Power* The life energy, or "chi," that each of us absorbs and releases. This energy sustains us.

4. *Divine Power* A combination of cosmic, Earth, and personal power. The source, the well, the power of the Goddess and God, the power that created everything.

The Three Steps of Magick

When you spin a spell, you create a magickal pattern. This pattern is a seed that you nurture and care for until it comes to fruition. In Wicca, the three basic aspects of every spell are: 1. intention and expectation, 2. desire, and 3. merging. Another way to see the steps is: 1. conceiving, 2. creating, and 3. experiencing.

You can apply the three steps to all spell crafting. First, you need to understand what your intentions are and what it is you expect, and most of all, that you really want it. Imagine your expectation coming true. In your mind, try it on like you would try on a pair of pants. Second, you need to have a strong desire for success. Third, you need to merge with Oneness, with divinity, as deeply as possible, and then a little deeper still, allowing your intention, expectation, and desire for success to flow out of you and into the world. Imagine releasing thought energy so strong that it becomes real!

Merging

Merging connects you with Oneness and is another cornerstone in successful spellwork. It is the natural feeling you get when you are in love, when walking on the beach at sunset, or when sitting next to an ancient redwood tree. Merging is the feeling you get when you are in tune and one with it all. It becomes your doorway to magick making. The deeper you merge, the more powerful your spells.

Oneness is everything, whatsoever it may be. By merging with Oneness in magick, you reach into the source, commune with the divine, and gather power for successful spells. Each of us is a part of Oneness. Merging with Oneness provides the conduit for making things happen.

When you merge with Oneness, you may experience sensations of relaxation, peacefulness, well-being, spinning, flying, whirling, lighthead-edness, or heaviness. You may feel like you are floating as you sense yourself being both every-thing and nothing, all at the same time. When you merge, you become one with everything, diffus-ing like a cloud into the universe.

You can enhance your merging experience by using breathing exercises, staring at candlelight, dancing, chanting, as well as listening to special music, drumming, and using visualization tech-niques.

The Goddess and God

Divine communion is a mainstay of all reli-gions, including Wicca. Divine guidance is a blessing and a boon. It is from deity that we de-rive sustenance. Wicca is open to most divine en-ergies that you might want to use in your magick. Work with deities to whom you feel the deepest connection.

Wiccans honor nature in the forms of the Triple Goddess (Maiden, Mother, and Crone) and the Horned God. For every aspect of the Goddess, there is an aspect of the God. Deities have solar, stellar, lunar, and earthly aspects and embody the Upper World, Middle World, and Underworld. One of the great powers of Wicca is that you are considered divine. You are Goddess! You are God!

In "The Witches' Creed," Valiente writes this of Lady and Lord:

> The Dark and the Light in succession,
> The opposites each unto each,
> Shown forth as a God and a Goddess:
> Of this did our ancestors teach.
> The Master and Mistress of magick,
> They dwell in the deep of the Mind,
> Immortal and ever-renewing,
> With power to Free or to Bind.

The female and male energies converge at conception. In Wicca, the Wheel of the Year mirrors the relationship of the Goddess and God. The Goddess fixes the God's nature to the seasons so that in the winter his bright nature sleeps while his dark nature roams the land. But after Yule his bright nature begins to awaken and fully awakens at the Spring Equinox. From there, his bright nature rules for the full season of the greening. When the green things come to fruit, and begin to die, his dark nature rules again, and his bright self enters his winter sleep.

Wicca concurs with the natural order of things. Male and female converge together into one, forming the basis for balance and harmony in our world. The female gives birth and is the vessel of creation. Within this context, all things, including the God, arise from the Mother.

Maiden, Mother, and Crone

The Triple Goddess of Maiden, Mother, and Crone represent the different aspects or faces of feminine energy.

The Maiden is unattached and full of potential. She is represented by the new and waxing moons. Examples of maiden goddesses are Caer (Celtic), Diana (Roman), and Athena (Greek).

The Mother is the giver of life: fertile, fruitful, nurturing, and protective. Represented by the full moon, examples are Anu (Celtic), Isis (Egyptian), and Gaea (Greek).

The Crone is experienced, knowledgeable, and wise. She offers guidance. Represented by the waning moon, examples are Kerridwen (Celtic) and Kali (Hindu).

"The Witches' Creed" says this of the Goddess:

She is youthful or old as she pleases,
She sails the torn clouds in her barque,
The bright Silver Lady of Midnight,
The Crone who weaves spells in the dark.

★ CHARGE OF THE GODDESS ★
(to be read aloud during magick making)

Whenever you have need of anything, once in the month and better when the moon is full, then shall you assemble in some secret place and adore the spirit of me, who am Queen of all witches. There shall ye assemble, ye who are fain to learn all sorcery, yet have not won its deepest secrets; to these will I teach all things that are as yet unknown. And ye shall be free from slavery; and as a sign that ye be truly free, you shall be naked in your rites; and ye shall dance, sing, feast, make music and love, all in my praise. For mine is the ecstasy of the spirit, and mine also is joy on earth; for my law is love unto all beings. Keep pure your highest ideals; strive ever toward them, let nothing stop you or turn you aside. For mine is the secret door that opens upon the Land of Youth, and mine is the cup of the wine of life, and the Cauldron of Cerridwen, which is the Holy Vessel of Immortality. I am the gracious Goddess, who gives the gift of joy unto the heart of man. Upon Earth, I give the knowledge of the spirit eternal; and beyond death, I give peace, and freedom, and reunion with those who have gone before. Nor do I demand sacrifice; for behold, I am the Mother of all living, and my love is poured out upon the Earth.

I am the beauty of the green earth, the white moon among the stars, the mystery of the waters, and the desire of the heart of man. Call unto thy soul, arise, and come unto me. For I am the soul of Nature, who gives life to the Universe. From me all things proceed, and unto me all things must return; and before my face, beloved of gods and of men, let thine innermost divine self be enfolded in the rapture of the infinite. Let my worship be within the heart that rejoicest; for behold, all acts of love and pleasure are my rituals. Therefore, let there be beauty and strength, power and compassion, honor and humility, mirth and reverence within you. And thou who thinketh to seek for me, know thy seeking and yearning shall avail thee not unless thou knoweth the mystery; that if that which thy seekest thou findest not within thee, thou wilt never find it without thee. For behold, I have been with thee from the beginning; and I am that which is attained at the end of desire.

Helpful Goddesses and Their Origins

Aife or Aoife (Celtic)   Consort of the sea god Manannan

Ailinn (Celtic)   Goddess of affection, romance, and love

Aine (Celtic)   Goddess of Earth and Sun, queen of the Faery folk; mate to Lugh

Airmed (Celtic)   Goddess of witchcraft and herb lore

Akupera (Hindu)   Goddess of moonlight

Anadyomene (Greek)   Sea-born goddess of sexuality

Andraste or Andrasta (Celtic)   Goddess of fertility, warriors, and victory

Anna Perenna (Roman)   Goddess of sexuality and fertility

Annapurna (Hindu)   Great Mother goddess of abundance; giver of plenty

Anu, Danu (Celtic)   Mother goddess of knowledge, healing, and fertility

Anuket or Anukis (Egyptian)   Goddess of the river and fertility

Aphrodite (Greek)   Goddess of love, pleasure, and beauty

Ardwinna (Celtic)   Goddess of the forests and woods

Arianrhod (Celtic)   Stellar and lunar goddess; her palace is the Corona Borealis, known as Caer Arianrhod (the Northern Crown)

Artemis (Greek)　Goddess of the moon and hunting; twin sister of Apollo

Artio (Celtic)　Goddess of fertility and wildlife; portrayed as a bear

Astarte (Assyro-Babylonian)　Great Mother goddess, associated with the planet Venus

Athena (Greek)　Goddess of wisdom and warriors in battle

Badb or Badhbh, Badb Catha, Bav, Bov, Bodhbh (Celtic)　Druidess of the Tuatha De Danann and goddess of war, inspiration, fury, and wisdom

Banba (Celtic)　Goddess of the sacred land

Bast (Egyptian)　Cat goddess of fertility, pleasure, dancing, music, and love

Belisama (Celtic)　Young goddess of fire whose name means "like unto flame" and "the bright and shining one"; wife of Belenus

Belisana (Celtic)　Goddess of healing, laughter, and the forests; associated with the Sun's warmth and woodland plants and animals

Blathnat (Celtic)　"Little Flower"; goddess of sex

Blodenwedd (Blodewedd, Blodeuedd) (Celtic) Beautiful and treacherous Sun and Moon goddess; associated with the white owl, the dawn, primroses, broom, cockle, oak, and meadowsweet

Bo Find (Celtic) Goddess of fertility

Boann or Boi, Boanna (Celtic) Mother of the herds; goddess of fertility, inspiration, and the river Boyn; wife of the Dagda

Branwen (Welsh) Goddess of love, called the White-Bosomed One and Venus of the Northern Sea; her name means White Raven

Bridget Brighid, Brede (Celtic) Fertility goddess of the Sacred Fire, the Sun, hearth, and home; the bride goddess of inspiration, poetry, medicine, healing, and smithcraft

Caer (Celtic) Swan maiden; wife of Angus

Cailleach (Pre-Celtic) Goddess of Earth, sky, Moon, and Sun, who controls the seasons and weather

Calliope (Greek) Muse of epic poetry

Cherubim (Hebrew) Goddess/god of sexuality and intercourse

Cilleac Bheur (Celtic)   Goddess of winter, whose staff can freeze the ground and wither the crops

Cliodna (Celtic)   Bird goddess and Faerie Queen associated with extraordinary beauty, shapeshifting, apples, and accompanied by three magickal birds

Coventina (Celtic)   Goddess of the well and the womb of the Earth; associated with healing springs, sacred wells, childbirth, renewal, and the Earth

Dana or Danu, Dannu, Anu, Ana, Anna, Ann, Don (Celtic)   The Mother goddess from whom Tuatha De Danann were descended; goddess of nature, wisdom, and creation

Deirdre (Greek)   "One who gives warning," or the older form Derdriu, "Oak prophet"; a humanized Goddess in the Red Branch tale of the exile of the sons of Uisnach; the daughter of the god Morgan

Demeter (Greek)   Goddess of fertility, marriage, and prosperity

Dia Griene (Celtic)   The daughter of the Sun

Diana (Roman)   Goddess of moonlight and the hunt

Edain or Etain (Celtic)   Goddess of beauty, grace, and wife of King Mider; one of the "White Ladies" of the Faery

Elayne or Elen, Elen Lwyddawg (Celtic)   Powerful goddess of leadership and war

Eostre or Ostara (Celtic)   Goddess of Spring and fertility

Epona (Celtic)   Goddess of fertility, power, and abundance

Eri of the Golden Hair (Celtic)   Goddess of love and sexuality

Erie (Eriu) (Celtic)   The triple Mother goddess of Erin, sometimes known as Ir, from which Ireland—the land of Ir—is derived; shapeshifter and goddess of sovereignty of the land

Fand (Celtic)   Shapeshifter and Faery Queen of Ireland; associated with the seagull

Findabair (Celtic)   Goddess of Connacht and the Otherworld; of beauty, grace, and love

Fliodhas (Celtic)   Goddess of the woodlands, protector of animals and forests; associated with the doe

Flora (Roman)   Goddess of fertility, sex, promiscuity, and spring

Fortuna (Roman)   Lady Luck; goddess of love and sexuality

Freya (Norse)   Goddess of love, beauty, passion, and fertility

Frigga (Norse)   Goddess of feminine arts; associated with hawks and falcons

Hathor (Egyptian)   Goddess of love, Mother of creation, and mistress of everything beautiful

Heket (Egyptian)   Frog goddess of childbirth and creation

Helen (Greek)   Moon goddess of childbirth, love, and fertility

Hera (Greek)   Goddess of matrimony

Hertha (Celtic)   Goddess of fertility, spring, the Earth, rebirth, and healing

Ishtar (Babylonian)   Goddess of love, beauty, and war; associated with Venus, the morning star

Isis (Egyptian)   Mother goddess; embodiment of femininity

Isong (African)   Goddess of fertility

Juno (Roman)   Goddess of matrimony

Kerridwen or Cerridwyn, Ceridwyn (Celtic) Goddess of knowledge and wisdom; she possessed the cauldron of inspiration

Kwan Yin (Oriental)   Goddess of compassion and beauty

Lakshmi (Hindu)   Goddess of beauty and good fortune

Letha (Celtic)   Midsummer harvest goddess

Macha or Emhain Macha (Celtic)   Threefold Sun goddess of fertility, war, and ritual games; associated with horse, raven, and crow

Maeve (Celtic)   Goddess of sexuality, fertility, and power

Maya (Hindu)   Goddess of creativity

Medb, Mab, Medhbh (Celtic)   Warrior queen and goddess of sex, fertility, and sovereignty

Mei or Mai, Meia (Celtic)   Mother of Gwalchmei; solar and Earth goddess

Meskhenet (Egyptian)   Goddess of childbirth

Modrona or Modron, Madrona, Matrona (Celtic) The Great Mother of Mabon (light)

Morgan Le Fay (Celtic)   Faerie Queen, sorceress, shapeshifter, and beautiful enchantress

Morgana (Celtic)   The Death Mother; goddess of war and fertility

Morrigan or Morrigana (Celtic)   "The Phantom Queen or Great Queen" and a sea goddess; she is the Triple Goddess of war who shapeshifts into a raven

Morrigu (Celtic)   Dark Gray Lady and Queen of the Sea; goddess of life, death, and magick

Nantosuelta (Celtic)   River goddess

Nemetona (Celtic)   Protectress of the sacred Drynemeton; warrior goddess of the oak groves and patron of thermal springs

Nephthys (Egyptian)   Goddess of dreams, divination, and hidden knowledge

Niamh or Neeve of the Golden Hair (Celtic) Goddess of love and beauty

Nimue or Niniane, Niviene, Nymenche (Celtic)
Student and teacher to Merlin, his consort

Omamama (Native American) The Cree ancestral goddess of beauty, fertility, gentleness, and love

Oshun (African) Goddess of love, pleasure, beauty, and dancing

Parvati (Hindu) Goddess of marital blessing

Penelope (Greek) Spring goddess of fertility and sexuality

Psyche (Greek) Goddess of love

Rhiannon (Celtic) Queen Mother, Queen Mare, or the Great Queen

Rosemerta (Celtic) Goddess of fertility, beauty, and love

Sadv (Celtic) Ancient deer goddess of the forests and nature

Selene (Greek/Roman) Moon and love goddess

Shakti (Hindu) Great Mother goddess, who embodies feminine energy

Sheila na Gig (Celtic)   Goddess of sex, birth, passion, and laughter

Sirona (Celtic)   Solar and astral goddess

Taillte (Celtic)   Earth goddess and foster mother to Lugh

Tiamat (Mesopotamian)   Great Mother goddess who took the form of a dragon

Tlazolteotl (Peruvian)   Goddess of love

Triana (Celtic)   The Triple Goddess; Sun-Ana, Earth-Ana, and Moon-Ana; also goddess of healing, knowledge, higher love, and wisdom

Var (Scandinavian)   Goddess of love

Venus (Roman)   Goddess of love and sexuality

Viviana or Vivian, Vivien (Celtic)   Goddess of love, birth, life, mothers, childbirth, and children; her consort is Merlin

Voluptas (Roman)   Goddess of pleasure and sensuality

The Horned God

The human antlered form has been a magickal image from the beginning of time, with horned deer becoming the animal prototype of the Horned God. Lord of the beasts, the Horned God rules the active forces of life and death, giving and taking in nature. He is the god of sexuality, hunting, and culling, and is associated with prosperity and wealth.

The Horned God is the wild, untamed principle in nature. A god of pleasure whose purpose is to purify through selection, so that the powers of fertility and growth will continue, he is also gentle and tender, protective, and comforting. His symbolic death is always in the service of life. Some of his names are Kernunnos, Pan, and Herne. In "The Witches' Creed," Valiente writes this of the Horned God:

By night he's the wild wind's rider,
The Horn'd One, the Lord of the Shades.
By day he's the King of the Woodland,
The dweller in green forest glades.

★ CHARGE OF THE GOD ★
(to be read aloud during magick making)

Listen to the words of the Great Father, who of old was called Osiris, Adonis, Zeus, Thor, Pan, Cernunnos, Herne, Lugh, and by many other names. My law is harmony with all things. Mine is the secret that opens the gates of life and mine is the dish of salt of the Earth that is the body of Cernunnos that is the eternal circle of rebirth. I give the knowledge of life everlasting, and beyond death I give the promise of regeneration and renewal. I am the sacrifice, the father of all things, and my protection blankets the Earth.

Hear the words of the dancing god, the music of whose laughter stirs the winds, whose voice calls the seasons. I who am the Lord of the Hunt and the Power of the Light, sun among the clouds and the secret of the flame. I call upon your bodies to arise and come unto me. For I am the flesh of the Earth and all its beings. Through me all things must die and with me are reborn. Let my worship be in the body that sings, for behold all acts of willing sacrifice are my rituals. Let there be desire and fear, anger and weakness, joy and peace, awe and longing within you. For these, too, are part of the mysteries found within yourself, within me, all beginnings have endings, and all endings have beginnings.

★

Helpful Gods and Their Origins

Adonis (Greek)   God of beauty, love, and vegetation

Aengus mac Og or Angus, Angus Og, Oengus (Celtic)   God of love and beauty; healer of souls; associated with romance and courting

Amaethon (Celtic)   Agriculture and harvest god called the Harvest King; associated with the fruits and tools of the harvest

Apollo (Greek)   Sun god of poetry, creative arts, music, healing, and divination

Arawn (Celtic)   Death, war, and ancestral god who was the King of Annwn, the Underworld; associated with the swine, magickal beasts, the ancestral tree, water springs, shapeshifting, and the cauldron

Bel/Baal (Assyro-Babylonian)   Sky god of fertility

Bhaga (Hindu)   God of marriage, fortune, and prosperity

Bel or Bile, Eel, Belenus, Belenos (Celtic)   Sun god of light and healing; referred to as "the Shining One"; husband of Belisama

Bodb Derg or Bodb the Red (Celtic) Son of Dagda and Boann; bard to the Tuatha de Danann and King of the Sidhe

Borvo or Bormo, Bormanus (Celtic) Healing god of unseen and concealed truth and inspiration through dreams; known as the golden god associated with hot springs and a golden harp

Bragi (Norse) God of poetry

Bran or Bron (Celtic) God of music and prophecy, protector of bards and poets; associated with singing, the bard's harp, and the Sacred Head

Bres (Celtic) God of fertility and agriculture

Buddha (Indian) The energy of knowledge and wisdom

Camulus (Celtic) God of war

Chandra (Hindu) God of fertility and the Moon

Chango (African) Great love god, drummer, dancer, king

Condatis (Celtic) Water god

Cordemanon (Celtic) God of knowledge, ancestry, and travel; associated with the Great Book of Knowledge, stone circles, and sacred sites

Creidne or Creidhne, Credne (Celtic)   Master swordmaker named "The Bronze Worker"; associated with smiths, wrights, metal-working, and craftspersons

Cupid (Roman)   God of love

Dagda (Celtic)   God of abundance, love, pleasure, and plenty

Dewi (Celtic)   The Red Dragon God, the emblem of Wales

Diancecht (Celtic)   God of herbalism, healing, and physician to the gods; associated with the mortar and pestle

Dionysus (Greek)   From pastoral beginnings, associated with goat herding; became the god of ecstasy, sex, revelry, and pleasure

Dumiatis or Dumeatis (Celtic)   God of creative thought and teaching

Dwyane (Celtic)   God of love

Dwyn (Celtic)   God of love and mischief

Eros (Greek)   God of passionate love

Esus (Celtic)   Woodland god associated with hunting, the sword, the Golden Bull (Tarvos), and the bow and arrow; pictured as a woodcutter

Fagus (Celtic)   Monadic god of all Beech trees

Frey (Norse)   God of fertility, joy, peace, and happiness

Geb (Egyptian)   Earth god, whose brother is Nut, the Sky god

Gobannon or Govannon, Goibniu, Goibhnie, Goibnll (Celtic)   The Divine Smith and god of magick; also called "Gobban the Wright" and Gobban Saer, "The Master Mason"

Gwalchmei (Celtic)   God of love and music; son of the goddess Mei

Gwydion (Celtic)   Shapeshifter and god of the arts, eloquence, kindness, and magick

Gwyn ap Nudd (Celtic)   God of the Otherworld, the death chase, and the Wild Hunt

Heimdall (Norse)   God of Light, known for his sight and hearing

Hellith (Celtic)   God of the setting sun and protector of souls of the dead

Hermes (Greek)   God of flocks and music; guides travelers; divine messenger

Hypnos (Greek)   Mesmerizing god of sleep and dreams

Jupiter (Roman)   God of the light sky; wielder of thunderbolts

Kama or Kamadeva (Hindu)   God of love; "Seed of Desire"

Kernunnos or Cernunnos (Celtic)   Father god of virility, prowess, and nature

Khons (Egyptian)   God of the Moon; father is Amon-Ra

Khnum (Egyptian)   God of fecundity and creation

Krishna (Hindu)   God of erotic delight and ecstasy

Llyr or Ler, Lir, Lear, Leer (Celtic)   Sea god of music and king of the oceans

Lugh (Celtic)   God of mastery, love, sex, and romance

Luchta or Lucta, Luchtaine (Celtic)   Carpenter god and shield-maker for the Tuatha De Dannan

Lugh or Lug, Lleu, Llew, Llaw, Gyffes (Celtic) Sun god and master of all arts; god of poets, bards, smiths, and war

Mabon or Mapon, Maponus (Celtic)   "The Divine Son" and "The Son of Light"; god of sex, love, magick, prophesy, and power

Manannan or Manannan ap Llyr, Manannan Mac Llyr (Celtic)   Shapeshifter, teacher; god of magick, the sea, and travel

Math, son of Mathonwy (Celtic)   Seasonal King God of magick, wisdom, enchantment, and sorcery

Mercury (Roman)   God of safe travel and communication

Merlin or Myrddin (Celtic)   Woodland and nature god

Mider or Midir (Celtic)   The Faery King, god of the Underworld and consort to Etain; bard and chess player; associated with the Isle of Man, the Faery hill of Bri Leith, and chess

Min (Egyptian)   God of sex, fecundity, and crops

Mitra (Hindu)   God of friendship

Nodens (Celtic)   God of dreams and sleep

Nuada or Lludd, Nudd, Lludd Llaw Ereint (Celtic)
The Good Father; first king of Tara; consort to
Fea, the war goddess, and to Morrigan

Nwyvre (Celtic)   God of space and the firmament;
consort to Arianrhod

Odin (Norse)   Father god of wisdom and inspiration

Ogma or Ogmios (Celtic)   "The Binder"; god of
eloquence, knowledge, and literature; Ogma in-
vented the Ogham Runes

Osiris (Egyptian)   Father god of civilization and
rebirth

Pan (Greek)   Nature god of lust, love, play, and
pleasure

Pryderi (Celtic)   Youthful shapeshifter god and
son of the goddess Rhiannon and the god Pwyll

Pwyll (Celtic)   Prince of Dyfed and King of the
Otherworld; a pack of hounds accompanies him

Ra (Egyptian)   Sun god; father of all gods; he has a detachable eye that can go off on its own

Robur (Celtic)   Forest King and Monadic tree god of the forests, particularly oaks

Shiva (Hindu)   God of creation; embodies masculine energy

Silvanus (Roman)   God of the forests and agriculture, especially around woodland clearings

Smertullos (Celtic)   The preserver and Lord of Protection; god of the abyss and the unmanifested

Sucellos (Celtic)   River god and twin to the Dagda; shapeshifter and god of fertility and death

Taliesin (Celtic)   Son of Kerridwen; poet, prophet, and bard

Tarvos Trigaranos (Celtic)   God of vegetation and virility

Tethra (Celtic)   Sea god of magick

Thoth (Egyptian)   God of writing; Moon-god; magickian

Tyr (Norse)   God of war and justice

Thor (Norse)   God of thunder; protector from chaos

Zeus (Greek)   The powerful leader of the gods of Olympus

★ ★ ★ Notes ★ ★ ★

★ ★ ★ Notes ★ ★ ★

★ ★ ★ Notes ★ ★ ★

CHAPTER TWO

A Time for Magick

Some days you get up and everything seems to work out for you. Have you ever wondered why? On those days, you get a feeling that you can do no wrong and that everything will go smoothly. These are the best days not only to go to Vegas but also to cast spells.

Familiarizing yourself with the best days, Moon and Sun phases, and astrological signs during which you should craft spells, adds power to your magick making as it increases the level of your success. Timing your spell casting formulas synchronizes your magickal goals with the natural energy of the elements, the seasons, and the universe.

Ideal times for magick making are the Full Moons, called Esbats, and the Sun festivals called Sabbats. You can always craft spells any time you need to, so don't let timing trip you up. Specifically, it's your intention and the depth of your merge that makes the magick happen. I suggest using common sense to keep your magickal timing practical.

The Best Time of Day for Spinning Spells

In addition to the timing of the Esbats and Sabbats, you will also find that your spells are more effective when you do them during certain times of the day. This timing is different for everyone. To discover the best time of day for you to do your spells, try spell casting at different times and then select the one that brings the best results. Remember there are no set rules. That is one of the beauties of Wicca.

Traditionally, just before dawn, noon, twilight, and midnight are considered to be the most auspicious times to do magick spells. These are the times of day when the veils between the mortal and divine worlds are most permeable. I prefer to craft my spells at noon, twilight, and after dark. I rarely cast spells just before dawn or at midnight (also called the Witching Hour) for the simple reason that I am usually asleep during these times.

Magickal Correspondences of the Days of the Week

Each day of the week has certain magickal energies and correspondences to the gods and astrology. These energies can be used to empower your spells. Below is a list of the days of the week, each day's ruling planet, and their spell crafting qualities.

Monday—Moon's Day (ruled by the Moon)

Spell Crafting Qualities: Dream magick, divination, finding employment, female fertility, psychic abilities, beginning projects, and voyages

Tuesday—Tyr's Day (ruled by Mars)

Spell Crafting Qualities: Defense, protection, courage, personal power, passion, business, conquering enemies, and breaking negative spells

Wednesday—Woden's (Odin's) Day (ruled by Mercury)

Spell Crafting Qualities: Divination, wisdom, learning, travel, business, creativity, communication, and psychic awareness

Thursday—Thor's Day (ruled by Jupiter)

Spell Crafting Qualities: Wealth, good luck, contracts, legal matters, expanding business, political power, friendship, lust, ambition, and male fertility

Friday—Freya's Day (ruled by Venus)

Spell Crafting Qualities: Love, romance, friendship, happiness, beauty, pleasure, musical skill, artistic ability, travel, and sexuality

Saturday—Saturn's Day (ruled by Saturn)

Spell Crafting Qualities: Protection, property, position, inheritance, agriculture, life patterns, structure, banishing, and resolution

Sunday—Sun's Day (ruled by the Sun)

Spell Crafting Qualities: Healing, success, prosperity, peace, harmony, friendship, dissolving negativity, and divine power

Moon Phases and Esbats

Moon magick is another essential element of spell crafting. Most Wiccans coordinate their spells with the cycles of the moon. This adds powerful lunar energy to spells. To find out which astrological sign and phase the moon is in, refer to an emphemerus or an astrology calendar. You can purchase one or find this information on the Internet.

Always reflect on the intent of the spell you are spinning before selecting the best moon phase. The phase of the moon that you spin your spells in depends largely upon your magickal goal. I avoid casting spells on eclipses of the moon: To do so often brings disastrous results because the lunar and solar ties are severed during eclipses. On the other hand, Blue Moons are particularly auspicious for spinning spells. The following table listing Moon phases and their magickal qualities will help you better craft your spells.

New Moon (the exact night of the new moon)

Spells for initiating new beginnings, new jobs, new relationships, new lovers, new ventures, and new ideas. This is also the time to craft magickal tools. The New Moon corresponds to the Maiden aspect of the Triple Goddess in Wicca.

Waxing Moon

Spells for growth, divination, love, healing, planting seeds, protecting animals, making changes, creating new associations, rekindling romance, forming friendships, attracting prosperity and abundance, increasing good luck, networking, and working on creative projects. The Waxing Moon corresponds to the Maiden aspect of the Triple Goddess in Wicca.

Full Moon (the exact night of the Full Moon)

Spells for love, inspiration, empowerment, creativity, dream magick, divination, healing, enhanced sexuality, fertility, prosperity, communication, shapeshifting, completing goals, and personal success. The Full or High Moon is the best time to cast all kinds of positive spells as the lunar energy is at its peak. The Full Moon corresponds to the Mother aspect of the Triple Goddess in Wicca.

Waning Moon

Spells for overcoming obstacles, protection, weight loss, ridding yourself of negative associations and situations, exorcism, overcoming addiction, dissolving ties, changing bad luck, breaking curses, and getting rid of bad habits. This moon corresponds to the Crone or Wise Woman aspect of the Triple Goddess in Wicca.

Dark or Black Moon (the three-and-a-half day period before the New Moon)

Spells for protection, shapeshifting for protection, and staving off negative magickal attacks. Many Wiccans avoid spinning spells on the Black Moon as this is the time when the lunar energies are at their lowest. The Black Moon corresponds to the Crone aspect of the Triple Goddess in Wicca.

Astrological Correspondences

Each month, the moon moves through the twelve astrological signs. These correspondences are traditionally used in timing spells. For example, love spells are especially effective when the moon is in Taurus and Libra. Apply the following astrological correspondences, along with their spell crafting qualities, to give your spells an extra boost of universal energy.

Aries (March 20–April 19)

Spell Crafting Qualities: Fire power, building personal strength, adventuring, persisting, activating new ventures, meeting challenges, getting things going

Taurus (April 19–May 20)

Spell Crafting Qualities: Creativity, love, fertility, security, sensual desire, determination, generating abundance, artistic inspiration, developing physical strength

Gemini (May 20–June 21)

Spell Crafting Qualities: Balancing polarities, communication, ideas, curiosity, compromise, connecting with spirit guides, sending messages, developing psychic abilities

Cancer (June 21–July 22)

Spell Crafting Qualities: Creating emotional balance, fertility, mothering, keeping secrets, protecting and blessing home and family, exploring past lives

Leo (July 22–August 22)

Spell Crafting Qualities: Expressing yourself, building magickal power, fathering, improving self-esteem, prowess, leadership, generosity, furthering your career, productivity

Virgo (August 22–September 22)

Spell Crafting Qualities: Organizing, structuring, improving employment, working with others, healing, attending to details, analyzing, serving others

Libra (September 22–October 23)

Spell Crafting Qualities: Discovering or enhancing romance, love and relationships, balancing energies, creativity, making new friends and partnerships

Scorpio (October 23–November 21/22)

Spell Crafting Qualities: Creativity, passion, shapeshifting, exploring mysteries, exploring past lives, moving past fear, inheritance, sex magick, divination

Sagittarius (November 21/22–December 21)

Spell Crafting Qualities: Expanding knowledge, changing perceptions, being optimistic, traveling, changing bad luck to good luck, exploring new places and new ideas, going on vision quests

Capricorn (December 21–January 19)

Spell Crafting Qualities: Practicality, discipline, giving order to your life, building ambition, developing patience, improving your public image, advancing your career, prosperity

Aquarius (January 19–February 18)

Spell Crafting Qualities: Using astrological knowledge, stimulating action, mysticism, delving into the unknown, inventing new concepts and things, promoting change, working with groups

Pisces (February 18–March 20)

Spell Crafting Qualities: Dream magick, enhancing intuition, connecting with the divine, using your imagination, ancestral communication, increasing healing powers

Magickal Moon Esbats

The moons of the year are called the Esbats in Goddess-based Wiccan traditions. Like the moon phases, the Esbats each have their own signature lunar energy, which can be used to your advantage in spell casting. "The Witches' Creed" says this of the Esbats:

Thirteen silver moons in a year are,
Thirteen is the Coven's array,
Thirteen times at Esbat make merry,
For each golden year and a day.

The thirteen moons also have magickal names. To figure out which Esbat matches which moon name, start counting the moons beginning with the first Full Moon after the Winter Solstice (usually on December 21 or 22). For example, if a Full Moon rises on January 3 in a given year, it would be the first Esbat called the Wolf Moon.

Some years have thirteen Full Moons while others have thirteen New Moons. This means that in some years, there isn't a thirteenth Full Moon. For easy reference, just check an emphemerus, astrology calendar, or the Internet for the date of the Winter Solstice and the Full Moons. The following table lists the Esbats, their Wiccan names, and their inherent lunar energies.

1st Esbat—Wolf Moon

Personal potential, loyalty, family, trusting your instincts, shapeshifting, developing clairvoyance, dream magick

2nd Esbat—Storm Moon

Polarities, duality, creating intensity, purification, getting rid of bad habits

3rd Esbat—Chaste Moon

Purification, natural balance, and the trinity of Maiden/Mother/Crone and Son/Father/Wise Man

4th Esbat—Seed Moon

Planting the seeds for attaining your magickal goals, starting projects, using the powers of the elements

5th Esbat—Hare Moon

Balancing your ego, improving your physical environment, fertility, growth, advancing toward your magickal goals

6th Esbat—Dyad Moon

Bridging the divine and the mundane, shapeshifting, divine gifts, prosperity, the sacred union between individuals

7th Esbat—Mead Moon

Altered states of awareness, dream magick, divine communication, healing, absolute fluorescence

8th Esbat—Wort Moon

Working with the natural cycles of things, putting ideas together, formulating spells

9th Esbat—Barley Moon

Increasing personal will, honing magickal skills, attaining magickal goals

10th Esbat—Wine Moon

Healing, divination, developing psychic abilities, divine inspiration, healing power

11th Esbat—Blood Moon

Ancestral communion, maternity, paternity, family, fellowship, divine oaths

12th Esbat—Snow Moon

Focusing on the divine within, making personal and professional changes, freezing out negativity

13th Esbat—Oak Moon

Rebirth, shapeshifting, metamorphosis, transformation, incarnation, transmigration

Sun Sabbats

"The Witches' Creed" says this of the Sabbats:

Four times in the year the Great Sabbat,
Returns, and the Witches are seen,
At Lammas and Candlemas dancing,
on May Eve and old Hallowe'en.

When day-time and night-time are equal,
When sun is at greatest and least,
The four Lesser Sabbats are summoned,
Again Witches gather in feast.

Wiccans traditionally celebrate eight Sun Sabbats that mark the progress of the Goddess and God through the year. The Sabbats are also referred to as the Quarter or Minor Sabbats (the Solstices and Equinoxes) and the Major or Cross-Quarter Sabbats (the four days that fall halfway between the Solstices and Equinoxes). The evening just before a Sabbat is the most powerful time for Wiccans to cast spells because the universal energy is at its peak.

Altogether, the eight Sabbats form the Wheel of the Year as they follow the path of the Sun through the seasons. In some Wiccan traditions, the Sabbats are exactly at 00.00 degrees and 15.00 degrees of the astrological Sun sign that they fall under. In modern Wiccan practice, each Sabbat also has a set date. For easy reference, I have listed the name, astrological degree, date, and spell crafting qualities of each of the eight Sun Sabbats.

Samhain

Also called Halloween, Hallowmass, and All Hallow's Eve (Cross-Quarter)
15.00 degrees Scorpio

Date: October 31
Marks the dark half of the year
Spell Crafting Qualities: (This is the time when the veil between the worlds is at its thinnest. One of the prime Sabbats for doing all kinds of magick, including divination, shapeshifting, astral travel, ancestral communion, honoring the dead, and working with the faeries.

Winter Solstice

Also called Yule (Quarter)
00.00 degrees Capricorn
Date: December 21 or 22
Shortest day and longest night of the year
Spell Crafting Qualities: Associated with the re-birth and blessings of the Sun; a time of letting the past go, of reflection, and building personal strength, protection, and integration.

Imbolg

Also called Imbolc, Bridget's Fire, Oimelc, and Candlemas (Cross-Quarter)
15.00 degrees Aquarius
Date: February 2
An annual time of birth
Spell Crafting Qualities: Associated with the sacred fire, which can be used to rekindle your magickal goals. Craft spells for fertility and updating your files. Start projects and think about what it is you really want to create in your life.

Spring Equinox

Also called Hertha's Day, Ostara, Oestara, Eostar (Quarter)
00.00 degrees Aries
Date: March 21 or 22
Day and night are equal
Spell Crafting Qualities: A time of balance, of planting seeds and ideas; fertility, combining elements, and bridging obstacles. The perfect time for learning from nature, communicating with your power animal, and shapeshifting.

Beltane

Also called May Day, Bealtaine, and Walpurgisnacht (Cross-Quarter)
15.00 degrees Taurus
Date: May 1
Marks the light half of the year
Spell Crafting Qualities: A time of youth and playfulness, personal growth, love, sexuality, increased fertility, and romance. One of the prime Sabbats with lots of fire energy for crafting powerful spells, especially love and prosperity spells.

Summer Solstice

Also called Midsummer, Letha's Day, and Litha (Quarter)
00.00 degrees Cancer
Date: June 21 or 22

Longest day and shortest night of the year
Spell Crafting Qualities: A time of absolute fluorescence, of honoring the ancestors and the faeries. The ideal time for forming new alliances with otherworldly beings such as the faeries, for shapeshifting and working with your power animals.

Lughnassad

Also called Lammas (Cross-Quarter)
15.00 degrees Leo
Date: First Week of August
An annual time of harvest
Spell Crafting Qualities: A time for mastering skills, joining together, handfastings, and harvesting your magickal goals.

Autumnal Equinox

Also called Hellith's Day, Modron, and Mabon (Quarter)
00.00 degrees Libra
Date: September 21 or 22
Day and night are equal
Spell Crafting Qualities: A time of balance. A pivotal point for attaining magickal goals, taking on new attitudes, setting things right, and paying off old debts.

★ ★ ★ Notes ★ ★ ★

★ ★ ★ Notes ★ ★ ★

★ ★ ★ Notes ★ ★ ★

CHAPTER THREE

Magickal Focals

The items used in magick, other than your tools, are called magickal focals or components. They help to focus, amplify, and enhance magickal powers. All items that you use should blend with the spell you are crafting. Food, music, scented oils, candles, incense, symbols, and other decorations, can all add more sensory power to your magick, bringing quick and successful results. The following types of focals can be used in spell crafting.

Visual Focals

Your sense of sight

Things you look at. For example, the pentacle and miniature broom that are included in this kit. Also, photographs, symbols, drawings, paintings, statues, and flowers.

Auditory Focals

Your sense of hearing

Sounds and noises you hear. Words of power, music, singing, chanting, drumming, humming, breathing, ocean, fountains, and birds.

Gustatory Focals

Your sense of taste

Food, beverages, herbs, the lips of your lover, and salt on skin.

Kinesthetic Focals

Your sense of touch

The tumbled quartz crystal included in this kit. Other examples are skin, plants, creatures, fabrics, magick tools, and shells.

Olfactory Focals

Your sense of smell

The lavender scented oil and smudging wand included in this kit. Also, scented candles, foods, essential oils, perfume, aromatic plants, flowers, herbs, and incense.

Intuitive Focals

Your sense of intuition

Ritual jewelry, medicine bags, antiques and/or heirlooms, talismans.

The Elements and Directions

The four elements of Earth, Air, Fire, and Water, and their directions of North, East, South, and West, play essential roles in the practice of Wicca. Everything—absolutely everything—works off the elements. Spirit, or the practitioner, is often considered the fifth element.

The element of the North is Earth, represented on the altar by a bowl of salt or soil. The Earth element grounds and stabilizes. In astrology, the Earth signs are Taurus, Virgo, and Capricorn, whose main traits are dependability, endurance, stubbornness, and practicality. Mastery of the Earth element gives you strength, structure, and understanding of the cycles of nature.

The East corresponds to the Air element, represented on the altar by the incense and censor. The element of Air can move through just about anything. In astrology, Gemini, Libra, and Aquarius are Air signs, whose main traits are sociability, perception, communication, and intellectual ability. Mastery of the Air element gives you detachment and the ability to move around or through anything. Earth is structured, while Air is fluid.

The South represents the Fire element, represented on the altar by the burning candle and candlestick. Fire is the element of action. The astrological Fire signs are Aries, Leo, and Sagittarius, whose main traits are expansion, personal drive, and energy. Mastery of the Fire element gives you immense transformational power and expanded creativity.

The West corresponds to the Water element, symbolized on the altar by the chalice of water. Water sustains life. It is fluid and flows. Water signs are Cancer, Scorpio, and Pisces, whose main traits are intuition, emotion, wisdom, and secrecy. Mastery of the Water element helps you flow toward your goals.

Spirit is at the center of the circle, or in all directions. It is that which connects all things into Oneness.

One way to strengthen your rapport with the elements is by associating them with different areas of your being. Repeat these words aloud several times each day.

My flesh and bones are the earth, the earth is my
flesh and bones, we are One.
My breath is the air, the air is my breath,
we are One.
My eyes are the light, the light is my eyes,
we are One.

My emotions are water, water is my emotions,
we are One.
I am spirit, spirit is me, we are One.
I am all elements, all elements are me,
we are One.

Words of Power

To be able to *spell* a word, to write it, and to be able to say it, is a form of magick all its own. Just ask any child learning the magick of reading and writing. Each letter has its own sound, form, and meaning. This is especially evident in runes, where each runic letter corresponds to the elemental forces of creation, life, and destruction.

Wiccans apply the power of language, thought, and the spoken word to their magick. Words of power, whether spoken aloud or thought as in prayer, are most effective when they are heartfelt and true to your intention. Doing invocations, blessings, affirmations, chants, and incantations helps you to focus on your magickal goal. Words of power also add to the overall ceremonial quality of spell crafting.

Examples of traditional words of power are spiritual texts such as "The Wiccan Rede," "The Charge of the Goddess," and "The Charge of the God." You can also use the wording you find in Wiccan books such as this one, or you can tweak the author's wording to better suit your circumstances. You can use pieces from poems or songs you especially like, or you can create original incantations, blessings, prayers, and affirmations, using your own words, poems, stories, other languages, and so forth. For example, a blessing can be as simple as "Blessed be!"

Color Correspondences

Along with words of power, the natural energies of color can greatly enhance your spell crafting. Representing yourself and/or the intention of your spell, color is a powerful visual component in magick. Focals used in spinning spells such as candles, flowers, ritual tools, and altar cloths all come in different colors. This can be used to your advantage.

Colors all have different harmonics, which influence energy. They set the stage, so to speak. For example, green candles are burned in prosperity spells because green is the color associated with money.

The following list is a basic guide for adding a rainbow of color to your magick. Remember, if a color means something else to you than what's on this list, go with what works. Select colors that feel right to you.

Silver

Peace, dream magick, ancestral communication, insight, clairvoyance, astral travel, divination

Gray

Mastery, divination, dream magick, balance, wisdom, merging, invention, discovery

White

Clarity, divine guidance, power, purity, love, motivation, truth, meditation, inspiration, peace, protection, Oneness

Blue

Purification, healing, divination, travel, loyalty, psychic protection, perception, divination, harmony, peace, moving energy, higher wisdom

Purple

Intuition, divination, consecration, offensive protection, dream magick, ancestral wisdom, spiritual healing, power, leadership

Pink

Romance, love, friendship, calming emotions, children, kinship, kindness, compassion

Rose

Ecstasy, divine love, enlightenment, romance

Red

Strength, survival, action, passion, lust, sexuality, vitality, virility, courage, rebirth, focus, power, animation, intense desire

Orange

Business, joy, generosity, success, comfort, prosperity, the home, friendship, happiness, meditation, justice, constructive action

Yellow

Mental agility, attraction, persuasion, imagination, knowledge, learning, teaching, understanding, truth, communication

Gold

Solar energy, wealth, increase, attraction, creativity, strength, security

Green

Abundance, fertility, originality, creativity, healing, birth, prosperity, regeneration, renewal, growth, nature, good luck

Brown

Pet and animal protection, stability, nurturing, rebirth, family, home, common sense

Black

Getting rid of negative energies, shifting negative energy to positive energy, closure, divination

Scented Oils

Oils are used in spell crafting in the form of ritual baths, sachets, charms, incense, as well as for anointing candles, consecrating tools and the altar, and anointing your body. The craft of making and using scented oils for magick purposes dates back before the rise of the Egyptian dynasty. Each oil has certain traditional qualities. Oils create a magickal state of awareness, especially when you use one particular scented oil in your bath, on the altar, on candles; for anointing, in sachets and charms, for consecrating tools, on correspondence, and on the gifts you give.

Oils can be very potent and care must be taken when using them. Be sure to do a skin patch test before using any oil on your skin. If you have any adverse reactions, immediately apply lavender oil, included in this kit, to soothe the skin. Discontinue using the oil that caused the reaction. If certain oils irritate your skin, an option is to put a drop or two of the oil on a cotton ball and carry it in your pocket. This way you can still take advantage of its magickal properties without harming yourself.

You can charge the vial of lavender oil in this kit as well as other scented oils you use for magick by rubbing the vial between your palms until the oil is warm. As you do this, imagine a bright beam of light moving from your hands into the oil, empowering it. Focus on the properties you would like in the oil, then imagine using the oil for successful spell casting. Do this for a few minutes. For a complete list of oils and their magickal qualities, refer to my book, *Love, Sex, and Magick* (Citadel Press, 1999).

Incense and Resins

Made by blending together herbs, spices, resins, gums, and oils, incense fills the air with magickal vibrations, and opens the higher centers of consciousness. For thousands of years, incense has appeared on altars as an offering to the gods and goddesses. It was burned in temples to purify the worshipers, and also represented the prayers of the faithful rising toward the heavens.

You can make your own incense or purchase ready-made sticks and cones. Be sure the incense you use matches your spell. Incense is also burned on charcoal blocks on the altar. These small disks are available from health food stores, Wiccan shops, and gift stores. Be careful not to burn your fingers when lighting the charcoal. Use a pair of tweezers to hold the charcoal disk while lighting it; I also recommend using a lit candle rather than a match or lighter to light the charcoal disk.

Set the lit disk into the bottom of your incense burner. Use a thin layer of pebbles, sand, or clean soil between the burner and the charcoal block. This will protect the burner. You can use powdered incense formulas prepared beforehand or you can sprinkle herbs on it, a pinch at a time, but be careful not to smother the lit disk. Then add drops of oil and small pieces of resin onto the burning herbs.

If you are sensitive to smoke, substitute essential oils and an aromatherapy diffuser. Putting a few drops of essential oil in a pan of boiling water or on a lightbulb also releases its power. For a variety of excellent incense recipes, refer to the book *Wicca Spell Crafting for Men* by A. J. Drew (New Page Books, 2001).

Crystals and Gemstones

Quartz crystals and gemstones act as natural energy magnifiers so they can be very useful in spell crafting. Each type of stone has certain energetic qualities that can be used in a myriad of ways from healing to shapeshifting. You can either purchase stones or find them in nature.

For more information about how to use stones for magick, please refer to my book *The Pocket Guide to Crystals and Gemstones* (Crossing Press, 1998). The following list are some examples of stones and their magickal qualities:

Amethyst Protection, healing, love, divination, astral travel, banishing nightmares, mental clarity

Carnelian Personal power, sexuality, creativity, past lives, protection, courage, focus, motivation

Citrine Mental quickness, dream magick, dispels negativity, insight, empowerment, shapeshifting

Clear Quartz The master stone for all magick; healing, divination, meditation, shapeshifting, astral travel, insight, higher consciousness, purification, protection, balancing energy

Diamond Strength, healing, empowerment, inspiration, protection, memory, prosperity, endurance, clarity

Emerald Sexuality, love, balancing emotions, patience, growth, healing, meditation

Garnet Friendship, faithfulness, strength, protection, virility, trust, balance

Jade Love, protection, wealth, purification, meditation, harmony, dispelling negativity

Lapis Lazuli Psychic development, divination, shapeshifting, empowerment, moving energy, knowledge, wealth, astral travel, creativity, protection

Malachite Shapeshifting, willpower, communication with nature, peaceful sleep, visions, healing, prosperity

Moonstone Moon magick, good fortune, fertility, love, lunar healing, receptivity, intuition, divination, artistic pursuits, balancing emotions

Pyrite Wealth, prosperity, plenty (To ensure prosperity, your piece of pyrite should hold together and not flake apart.)

Rose Quartz Friendship, love, romance, balances emotions, divine inspiration, adapting to change, forgiveness, faith, fertility, compassion

Ruby Strength, power, protection, insight, creativity, passion, friendship, clarity, astral travel, activates the life force

Turquoise Astral travel, dream magick, communication with your ancestors, elemental wisdom, motivation, healing, faery magick

Magick Symbols

Symbols are a form of magickal shorthand. You can use them to open the circle or carve them on candles and tools. You can also use them in spells, to consecrate objects, in divination, and for personal empowerment.

You are continuously encircled by symbols. Symbolism occurs with the process of association. Magick symbols have a layered quality, representing collections of thoughts and feelings. One thing gives meaning to another, with personal experience adding another valence to symbols. When people for hundreds—if not thousands—of years focus on a symbol, it gives it power. A very real field of energy is created around it. Whenever you use that symbol, you are tapping into that energy.

You can use traditional magick symbols or create your own. Many of those who practice the Craft also use a symbol together with their signature for protection and empowerment. I recommend doing this. Also, I suggest you familiarize yourself with the meaning of specific symbols before using them in order to correctly access their power. The following are some basic magick symbols.

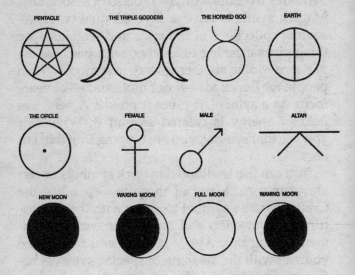

PENTACLE   THE TRIPLE GODDESS   THE HORNED GOD   EARTH

THE CIRCLE   FEMALE   MALE   ALTAR

NEW MOON   WAXING MOON   FULL MOON   WANING MOON

Magick Potions

A magick potion is a blend of herbs or other ingredients that have been steeped in water for magickal purposes. The basic ingredients used in making potions can be gathered, grown, or purchased. Most modern synthetic drugs are artificial replications of natural herbs and potions used by witches for thousands of years.

Each potion ingredient has a traditional magickal quality that makes it useful. Some potions such as teas are consumed, while others, such as powders and waters, are not. Potions can also be used to empower your spells.

When you begin making potions of your own, use an already existing potion recipe, and then modify it slightly by adding a safe ingredient that you know will improve the potion. Notice what effect this new ingredient has on the quality of the potion. Take it a step at a time, adding or subtracting one ingredient, and then check what effect the new ingredient has on the overall affect of the potion. Never use ingredients that are poisonous or that can cause harm to yourself or anyone else.

When you make your potions be sure to enchant or charge them. Do this by focusing your mind on the specific effect you expect the potion to have. Use your intention plus the natural energy of the ingredients. Your focussed energy is imparted into the ingredients through your willful intent, your touch, and the heat of your hands. When you make a potion, make it with the intention and expectation of imparting your goal into it.

Magick potions can be used for many practical things, from making you more creative and stimulating your senses, to bringing more love and prosperity into your life. The following love potion recipe is from my book, *The Witch and Wizard Training Guide* (Citadel Press, 2001). It is simple but effective.

Venus Water

Ingredients
   1 cup water
   3 roses
Preparation and Use
Pull off the rose petals one at a time, all the while empowering them with your intention. Then put them in a pot with the water. Simmer slowly for about fifteen minutes, and then let the liquid cool. Strain the water and put it in a container. Sprinkle the water in your bedroom, on your person, around your working space, in your car, or anyplace where you would like to encourage more love.

For a wealth of potion recipes, refer to *A Witch's Beverages and Brews* by Patricia Telesco (New Page Books, 2001).

Candle Magick

Ever since we discovered how to make fire, warming the coldness and lighting up the darkness, we have been fascinated by its power. The element of fire has been a part of magick making since the earliest of times. A symbol of purification and change, it is a potent power in spell crafting.

The power of fire is reflected in the Wiccan practice of candle magick. It is also one of the easiest forms of magick to practice and just requires candles and your focused mind. Most candle magick is done after dark.

Candles can be found just about everywhere. They come in all colors, shapes, and sizes, and have been a part of magick rituals since the earliest times, primarily because they burn with the power of fire. Each candle is unique with its own personality when lit, which is communicated by the Fire element, personified as a small salamander encased within the flame.

In spell crafting, candles speak a magickal language. Their words are the flickering flame, popping wax, and curling smoke. A candle flame touches something deep within your being. It represents the spirit's highest potential while the smoke carries your wishes, prayers, and desires to the divine.

Candle magick can be as simple as dedicating a candle to a God or Goddess, or making a dedication by lighting a candle in memory of an ancestor or for a friend who has died. Birthday candles are still used for making magick wishes.

Color, oils, symbols, and crystals can all be applied in candle magick. First pick the candle color that matches your spell. Then it's always a good idea to wash the candle(s) in cool salt water to rid them of any unwanted energies. You can use a quill, ballpoint pen, awl, toothpick, or any other pointed tool to inscribe candles. Make sure you consecrate the tool by dedicating it to the Goddess and God.

After you are done inscribing the candle, you can dress it with oil. Anoint the candle body with scented oil (match the scent to your goal). Start at the center of the candle and rub the oil all over both ends. As you do this, focus on the successful result of your spell. Always wipe any oil off your hands before lighting candles.

Once lit, spell candles are almost always allowed to burn down completely on their own. Because of this, make certain you have a fireproof holder and surface, where the candle can burn down in complete safety away from curtains, paper, and upholstery. If you don't want to leave the candle burning, use a candlesnuffer to put out the candle, and then relight the next day, so it can burn all the way down. Please refer to Chapter Five for easy-to-spin candle magick spells.

Once completely burned, beeswax candles can

be buried, while those made from synthetic materials should be put in the garbage. Also, remember not to use broken, chipped, or cracked
candles for magick, or your magick will come out
the same way.

★ ★ ★ Notes ★ ★ ★

★ ★ ★ Notes ★ ★ ★

★ ★ ★ Notes ★ ★ ★

CHAPTER FOUR

Setting Up Your Altar

As the Goddess's sacred table, the altar helps you connect with your spiritual nature. It is an outward expression of your personal relationship with the divine, and as such, serves as a sacred working surface that holds your magickal tools and spell components.

Altar means "high place," which is symbolic more of attitude than altitude. A connecting place where the sacred and mundane meet, your altar can be used for magick making, meditation, ritual, and prayer. Just approaching the altar with its tools, lit candles, and burning incense, immediately creates a feeling of magick.

When making your altar, I recommend using a sturdy surface such as a table, trunk, bureau drawer, or fireplace mantle. Benches, patio tables, large stones, a tree stump, or the ground can all be used as outdoor altars. It is customary for each person using the altar to contribute something.

Altar cloths are used to dress the altar surface and to protect it from dripping wax. Altar cloths can be made of any fabric, but natural fabrics, such as cotton, linen, silk, and wool, are always a good choice. Traditionally red or green, the altar cloth can be any color. It also doesn't have to be new. For example, the cloth could be the old lace dresser scarf your grandmother gave you. You can change your cloth regularly to match your magick making. Many Wiccans also decorate their altar cloths with embroidery or paint magick symbols like pentacles, stars, spirals, moons, and runes, on them.

I encourage you to change your altar with the changing seasons and holidays. For example, in the spring, put fresh flowers like daffodils and tulips on the altar. In the summer, put roses on it. At Yule, decorate the surface with mistletoe, evergreen boughs, and pine cones.

If you are going to leave your altar set up, situate it in a quiet spot where it won't get knocked over. You can also put your altar away when you are not using it. Traditionally, the altar cloth is used to wrap the altar tools, which are then placed in a special wooden box for safe keeping.

To make your altar less conspicuous, set it up on a bookcase shelf in your bedroom. If you have the opportunity and desire, you can make your entire home and property into a large altar. When you become adept at magick, you will find that every thought, every act, every living being, every object, everything becomes sacred, and life becomes your altar.

Cleansing and Blessing Your Altar

You can burn smudge (included in this kit) or ring a bell three times in each of the four directions, to cleanse and bless your altar. As you do this, ask the spirits of the four directions—North, East, South, and West—to guard your sacred space. Also ask the Goddess and God to bless your sacred space with their divine presence while you do magick. Always thank them for their divine presence.

Another way to cleanse and bless your altar is by putting sea salt in a bowl of water. Then take a sprig of greenery, dip it into the salt water, and lightly sprinkle your altar and ritual area in a clockwise motion as you say something like,

> Begone from here all evil and foulness.
> Begone from this place in the Lady's Name!

Say this three times while visualizing a white light edged in cobalt blue energetically cleansing the area. Then ask the Goddess and God to bless your sacred space. If you like, you can substitute the names of a specific Goddess and God, for example, the Celtic Kerridwen and Kernunnos, instead of saying Lady and Lord.

The Magickal Tools of Wicca

Before beginning your spell crafting, you set your altar with everything you will need. Much like a dinner table with its tablecloth, knives, forks, spoons, plates, glasses, and so forth, the Wiccan altar also has its implements such as the altar cloth, athame, wand, pentacle, bowl, chalice, and candles.

The magickal tools that you gather together, make, consecrate, and use regularly in spell crafting are more than symbols that trigger your subconscious. They are essentially a part of you, imprinted with your energy, and an extension of yourself. This is why I strongly suggest that you avoid letting other people play with or use your magickal tools. Always cleanse and consecrate each new tool before you use it for magick making. The following is a basic list of Wiccan tools you can collect, make, or purchase.

Athame   A double-edged knife, symbol of creative fire, used to cut the magick circle, cut magickal foods, to inscribe candles, and to carve runes. In "The Witches' Creed" Valiente writes,

When drawn is the Magickal circle,
By sword or athame or power,
Its compass between two worlds lies,
In the Land of Shades for that hour.

Most Wiccans dull the edges of ritual athames as a safety precaution. (Remember to keep all knives in a safe place, away from children.)

Bell A symbol of the Goddess, the bell is usually rung three times at the beginning and ending of a spell or ritual, to summon divine energies and for protection.

Bolline A knife with a white handle used to harvest herbs and slice foods, not normally used for rituals or actual spell casting.

Book of Shadows Your personal journal of spells, rituals, potions, thoughts, and ideas.

Bowl Representing Earth and the North point, you can put clean soil or the universal purifier salt, dry or mixed with water in your altar bowl.

Broom A miniature witch's broom or besom (pronounced beh-sum) is included in this kit. Used for protection, purification, astral travel, and fertility, witch's brooms were once made of wooden staffs and fans of feathers. Now made of straw or herbs tied around a branch of wood, use your broom to clean your altar and magick circle of unwanted energies. Used for Handfastings and fertility rituals, the broom staff is male, while the broom straw is female, again signifying the union of the God and Goddess. Lay your miniature broom on the left side of the altar. If you'd like to make a larger witch's broom for sweeping your magick circle, please refer to my book, *The Witch and Wizard Training Guide* for detailed instructions.

Candles and Candlesticks Often dressed (covered) with oils, candles represent the Fire element. Match the candle color to your magickal goal. Altar candles may be reused for magick, while ritual candles are used for specific rituals or spells and allowed to burn all the way down. Candles are always snuffed or pinched out rather than blown out. Candlesticks can be made of metals like brass and silver, or clay, glass, and so forth. The candle (male) and candlestick (female) also represent the God and Goddess.

Cauldron Symbol of the womb of the Goddess, the cauldron is a three-legged pot with its opening smaller than its base. Mostly used for scrying when filled with oil or water, and for holding candles and herbs. Large cauldrons are customarily put on the floor below the left side of the altar.

Chalice or Cup The symbol of Water, the chalice holds water or wine. Usually made of stoneware, clay, silver, lead-free pewter, or glass.

Cord Symbol of the umbilical cord, it is often nine feet in length and used to outline a magick circle or pentacle on the ground. You can also wrap it around the waist of your robe or cloak. Colored cords are used in cord magick.

Crystals and Gemstones A clear quartz stone comes in this kit. Clear quartz can be used for healing, love magick, dream magick, shapeshifting, and personal power. Each type of stone has its own signature energy that can be applied to spell crafting.

Drum Symbol of Air and Earth, the drum is a bridge to the spirit world. Drumming creates an altered state of consciousness and is used for astral travel, shapeshifting, working with your power animals, and ancestral communication.

Jewelry Ritual jewelry often include moon crowns, pentacles, amber or jet necklaces, or a ring with moonstone, opal, or carnelian set in silver. Ritual jewelry is generally only worn during magick making.

Incense Censor With Incense Symbol of Air and Fire when lit, incense smoke attracts helpful spiritual powers. Substitute an aromatherapy diffuser with essential oil if you are sensitive to incense smoke. A thurbile is a three-legged incense burner.

Mirror Used for divination, a witch's mirror is covered with a black drape when not in use. Your mirror can be a large hand-held mirror, a black scrying mirror, or a large piece of polished obsidian stone.

Mortar and Pestle Symbols of the Goddess (mortar) and God (pestle), these tools are used to grind herbs for spell crafting. They must be cleaned thoroughly between uses.

Oils and Herbs Representing the many deities and all of the elements, both herbs and essential oils have magickal properties that can empower spell crafting.

Pentacle One of the magickal components of this kit, and the most popular Wiccan symbol used on the altar and often worn as jewelry. The pentacle today is what the peace sign was in the 1960s. A pentacle is a pentagram (five-pointed star) that is surrounded by a circle. It is used for protection, power, and to attract the elemental powers of Earth, Air, Fire, Water, and Spirit.

Robe or Cloak Your robe or cloak can be made of any fabric, any color, and any design. Like a magickal skin, your robe or cloak is reserved for magick making.

Staff A symbol of authority, your staff is usually at least shoulder high. It is used to direct power like a wand. Sometimes viewed as a combination of the sword (Fire) and wand (Air), staffs are named for particular Goddesses and Gods such as Lugh's Staff.

Sword   Tool of command and fire, the sword is used to cut the circle, ancestral communication, and focusing your magickal will.

Talisman   The quartz crystal in this kit can be made into a talisman by following the step-by-step directions in Chapter Five. Carry your talisman and place it on the altar during spell casting to help you attain your magickal goals.

Wand   Associated with Air and made from wood, the wand is the witch's rod of authority and power and usually no longer than the length of your forearm. It can be used for invocation, banishing, and directing power. It is an extension of your body, in particular, your power hand. For step-by-step instructions for making your own magick wand, please refer to my book *Exploring Celtic Druidism* (New Page Books, 2001).

Cleansing, Consecrating, and Charging Your Tools

The three "C"s of magickal tool maintenance are cleansing, consecrating, and charging.

Cleansing

Smudge a new or used tool when you first acquire it to clear out any unwanted energies. You can use the smudge stick that comes with this kit, or you can purchase larger sticks at Wicca, health food, and New Age stores. Sandalwood incense smoke also works well as a cleansing agent as does sprinkling your tools with dew drops at sunrise on an Esbat or Sabbat morning. You can also use salt or salt water to rid your tools of unwanted energies, but be careful as salt can be corrosive.

Consecrating

To consecrate a tool, bless it with each of the elements: Earth (salt or soil), Air (incense), Fire (flame), Water (water), and Spirit (scented oil or crushed herbs). Actually apply the element to the tool. For example, sprinkle salt on a new athame, then pass it through incense smoke, the candle flame, sprinkle it with water, and rub it with scented oil. When doing this, say something like,

With this element of (fill in the blank,
for example, salt),
I consecrate and bless this tool
Great Mother Goddess and Father God
Drive out all impurities and empower this tool
Blessed be the Lady and Lord! Blessed be!
So shall it be!

Charging

To charge a tool, hold it in your hands and present it to each of the four directions, moving slowly in a clockwise circle. Then face the altar, and say something like,

I charge this magickal tool with the divine power
Of the Great Mother Goddess and All
Father God
By the powers of the sun, moon, stars,
and universe
By the powers of Earth, Air, Fire, Water,
and Spirit
May this tool serve me well and help me attain
my desires.
I ask that you charge this tool with your power
Old Ones!
I ask for your blessings. As I will, so shall it be!

Altar Layouts

Many Wiccans, like myself, set their altar up in the North quarter because the North represents Earth and that is where we find ourselves, on Earth. North is also the direction of divine wisdom and our ancestors. Many other Wiccans set the altar in the East quarter, which corresponds with the rising sun. Many others place the altar at the central hub area, within the center of the cir-

cle, where the four quarters connect together. I
suggest that you use your intuition and try a few
different spots, then choose the directional quarter and spot that feels the best to you.

To figure out the four directional quarters of
any given area, use a compass to mark the four
points of North, East, South, and West. Then divide the area into four, equal, pie-like pieces (not
necessarily round), using the four directional
points as midpoints in each of the pie pieces. The
North point will be at the center of the pie piece
for North, the East point is at the center of the pie
piece for East, and so on.

You can use the components in this kit, plus
three candles, a cup, and a bowl, to set up a simple, basic Wiccan altar. Start by putting two candles, one on the left and one of the right, on the
altar. These represent the feminine and masculine
energies of nature. Put the pentacle at the center
of the altar table. Then put a candle, its color corresponding to the season, above the pentacle. A
cup or chalice filled with wine or juice and the
miniature broom all go on the left side of the pentacle. Also put a bowl of water on the left side of
the pentacle. Put the smudge wand, a bowl of
salt, and your athame (if you have one) on the
right side of the pentacle. Refer to the following
altar diagram.

```
+-----------------------------------------------------------+
|                                                           |
|   Candle                              Candle              |
|                                                           |
|                      Candle                               |
|   Cup of Water       Pentacle         Bowl of Salt        |
|   Quartz Crystal                      Smudge Wand         |
|   Miniature Broom                                         |
|                                                           |
|                                       Athame              |
|                                                           |
+-----------------------------------------------------------+
```

Other Wiccans often place images of the Goddess and God on the altar and cast their spells before them. The left side is the creative, nurturing side, so this is where you put your image of the Goddess. Put your image of the God on the right, the power side of the altar. The athame is a male, fire tool and goes on the right side of the altar, while the chalice is a female, water tool and goes on the left side. Refer to the following altar diagram.

```
+-----------------------------------------------------------+
|            Goddess                    God                 |
|            Image                      Image               |
|                                                           |
|         Green Candle                  Red Candle          |
|                          Pentacle                         |
|                          Wine                             |
|    quartz crystal        White Candle                     |
|    Water                 Bowl          Incense            |
|    (Chalice)             (Salt)        (Burner)           |
|    Miniature broom                                        |
|            Wand                    Athame                 |
+-----------------------------------------------------------+
```

Many Wiccans divide their altar surface into the four quarters of North, East, South, and West, and their corresponding elements of Earth, Air, Fire, and Water. If you choose to do so, here are some basic altar suggestions.

• North quarter: Crystals and stones, a bowl of salt or earth, and pentacle

• East quarter: Incense and burner, a wand, feather, bell

• South quarter: Candle and holder, firepot, a sword or athame

• West: Chalice or cup of water, sea shell, moon symbol

Refer to the altar diagram below.

	North	
	Bowl of Salt	
	Pentacle	
	Crystals and Stones	
W Chalice or Cup		Incense **E**
e Sea shell		Wand **a**
s Moon Symbol		A Feather **s**
t		Bell **t**
	Candle	
	Athame or Sword	
	Firepot	
	South	

You can also add a besom, cauldron, tarot cards, runes, and your Book of Shadows to your altar. Miscellaneous items such as car keys, coffee cups, and groceries are not placed on the altar unless they are a part of your magick making. Use your common sense when setting up your altar so you can easily reach the items on it.

Drawing the Magick Circle

The magick circle is a energetic meeting ground where you can commune with the Goddess and God. It also protects you from negative influences when doing magick. After you set up your altar, it is time to cast or scribe the circle. You will need a compass, athame (or you can use your index finger), and bell. Follow these five easy steps.

1. Use the compass to find North.

2. Face North and slowly spin in a clockwise circle, with your arms stretched outward. As you are doing this, imagine a clear blue light washing out the area.

3. Say something like,

> May all evil and foulness be gone from
> this place.
> I ask this in the Lady's name.
> Be gone, now and forevermore!

4. Ring the bell three times.

5. Use your athame to draw a circle in the air around your magick making area. To do this, point it at the North point. Imagine a blue-white flame coming out of the tip of the blade, and creating a bright circle of light. You can use the index finger of your power hand in place of the athame by visualizing the light flaring from your fingertip.

   Knock three times on the altar surface with your wand or knuckles, in three series of three, in honor of the Triple Goddess. Your magick circle is now drawn. While in the circle, always move clockwise so the helpful energies are not accidentally banished.

Consecrating the Water and Salt

Take the chalice or cup of water from the altar and dip your athame tip into the water. Imagine the water being purified of all unwanted energies, and say something like,

O Creature of Water
Blessing upon thee
Cast out from thee all impurities and
uncleanliness
Of the spirits of phantasm
In the names of the Lady and the Lord
So mote it be!

Next, put the tip of your athame into the bowl of salt and imagine all negative energies flowing out of the salt. Say something like,

> O Creature of Earth
> Blessings upon thee
> Let all malignancies and hindrances pass forth
> Let all goodness enter and help me in my work.
> In the names of the Lady and the Lord
> So mote it be!

Then put three pinches of salt on your athame and put them into the chalice of water, one at a time. After you do this, say something like,

> As we are ever mindful
> That as water purifies the body,
> So salt purifies the spirit.

Stir the salt into the water in a clockwise motion with your athame. Wipe the blade dry, and say something like,

> Wherefore I do bless thee
> In the names of the Lady and the Lord
> That thou mayest aid me.

Cleansing the Circle

Take the chalice of saltwater and lightly sprinkle the altar three times. Then starting in the North quarter and moving clockwise, lightly sprinkle the

consecrated water three times at each quarter.
Finally sprinkle the water three times above and
three times below.

Consecrating the Fire and Air

Light the altar candle and say something like,

O Creature of Fire
Blessings to thee
I charge thee to allow no evil to defile this circle
In the names of the Lady and the Lord
So mote it be!

Take the incense and light it from the candle
flame. Extinguish the incense flame and watch
the smoke curl upward. Say something like,

O Creature of Air
Blessings to thee
I invoke thee to protect this our circle with love.
In the names of the Lady and the Lord
So mote it be!

Next, take the incense and cense the circle by
drawing, in the air, the elemental cross that corresponds with each quarter. For example, start
drawing the cross with the north arm in the
North quarter, the east arm in the East quarter,
and so forth. Finish at the center, using a three di-
mensional elemental cross.

ELEMENTAL CROSS

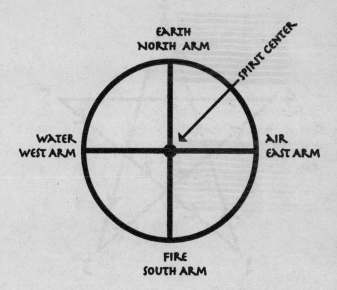

The elemental cross is an equal-armed cross derived from an ancient symbol known as a Sun Wheel.

INVOKING PENTAGRAM

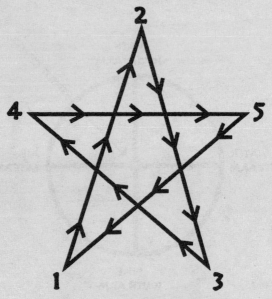

(Start and end at number 1)

TO DRAW A NORTH-ARMED CROSS

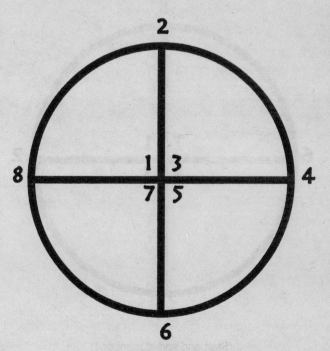

(Start and end at number 1)

TO DRAW AN EAST-ARMED CROSS

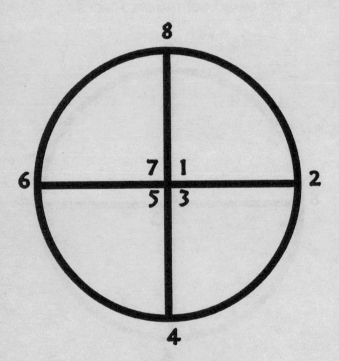

(Start and end at number 1)

TO DRAW A SOUTH-ARMED CROSS

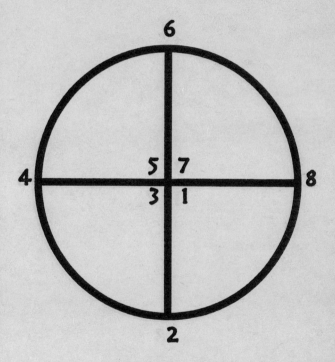

(Start and end at number 1)

TO DRAW A WEST-ARMED CROSS

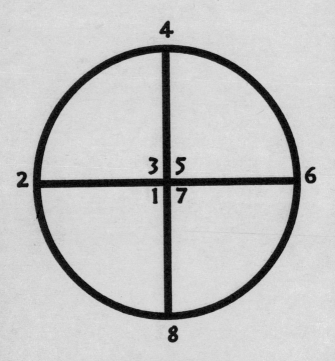

(Start and end at number 1)

THREE-DIMENSIONAL ELEMENTAL CROSS

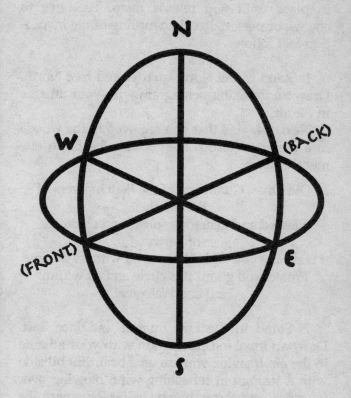

Imagine you are drawing the cross in three worlds as you do this. Go back and front around the middle.

Invoking the Elemental Guardians

Once you cast the circle, it is time to invoke the elemental powers. This sets a guardian at each directional ward of your circle while you do your spell crafting. These elemental guardians remain in place until you release them. Feel free to change or personalize the wording of the invocation that follows.

1. Stand in the North quarter and face North. Draw an invoking pentagram with your athame in the air.

Next, imagine that you are deep in the woods in a magickal forest. Merge with the Earth element, and say,

Old Ones, Guardians of the Watchtowers of
the North,
Blessed and generous spirits and creatures
of Earth,
I welcome you and ask that you witness this rite
Protect and guard this circle and all within.
Hail and Welcome!

2. Stand in the East quarter and face East. Draw an invoking pentagram with your athame in the air. Imagine you are on a beautiful hillside with a strong but refreshing wind blowing over your face and through your hair. Merge with the Air element, and say,

INVOKING PENTAGRAM

Old Ones, Guardians of the Watchtowers of
the East,
Blessed and generous spirits and creatures of Air,
I welcome you and ask that you witness this rite
Protect and guard this circle and all within.
Hail and Welcome!

3. Then stand in the South quarter and face southward. Use your athame to draw an invoking pentagram. Imagine yourself lying in the sun, soaking in its radiant warmth. Merge with the Fire element, and say,

Old Ones, Guardians of the Watchtowers of
the South,
Blessed and generous spirits and creatures
of Fire,
I welcome you and ask that you witness this rite
Protect and guard this circle and all within.
Hail and Welcome!

4. Then stand in the West quarter, facing westward, and draw an invoking pentagram with your athame. Imagine you are sitting next to a pristine mountain lake, or if you prefer, by the ocean. Merging with the powers of Water, say,

Old Ones, Guardians of the Watchtowers of
the West,
Blessed and generous spirits and creatures
of Water,

I welcome you and ask that you witness this rite
Protect and guard this circle and all within.
Hail and Welcome!

5. Now stand in the center of your magick circle, draw the invoking pentagram while pointing your athame above and then draw the invoking pentagram while pointing below. Face your altar, and say,

Generous spirits and creatures of Earth, Air, Fire, and Water
Grant me your power and protection tonight.
Hail and Welcome! Blessed be!

Binding the Circle

Walk clockwise, retracing the circle you have drawn. Reinforce and bind its energies by saying something like,

I cast this circle as a place of protection
and power,
A place between worlds and beyond,
In a time outside of time,
Where mortal and divine may meet.
May the Goddess and God bless and protect us.
Blessed be! So mote it be!

Calling Upon the Goddess and God

Honor the Goddess and God by inviting them into your circle. Do this by facing North and saying something like,

Lady and Lord
I welcome your loving presence into this circle
May you guide, bless, protect, and watch over
this circle
Blessed be! So mote it be!

Cutting the Little Gate

If you need to leave the circle during magick making, cut a doorway (called the little gate) with your athame. This is an energetic doorway. Then exit the circle using this gate, making sure you seal the doorway with your athame when you leave. Reverse the process to get back in the circle. Whenever possible, cut the doorway at a physical door, so you can easily come and go. Now that the circle is cast, it is time for you to do your spell crafting. Please refer to Chapter Five for step-by-step instructions.

Bidding Farewell to the Goddess and God

When you are done casting your spells, face North, and say something like,

Thank you Lady and Lord for watching over
this circle
I ask for your blessings and love
Please depart in peace. Hail and Farewell!

Banishing the Four Quarters

Once you are done with your magickal works,
banish the four quarters. To do this, begin in the
North quarter and move clockwise through the
four quarters. Stand in the North, draw a banishing pentagram with your athame or index finger
of your power hand. Say something like,

Generous powers of Earth, depart in peace.
Many thanks for your presence.
Hail and Farewell! Blessed be!

Then stand in the East, draw a banishing pentagram, and say,

Generous powers of air, depart in peace.
Many thanks for your presence.
Hail and Farewell! Blessed be!

Next, move to the South quarter, draw a banishing pentagram, and say,

Generous powers of Fire, depart in peace.
Many thanks for your presence.
Hail and Farewell! Blessed be!

BANISHING PENTAGRAM

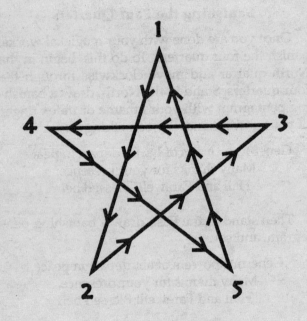

(Start and end at number 1)

Then stand in the West quarter, draw a banishing pentagram, and say,

> Generous powers of Water, depart in peace.
> Many thanks for your presence.
> Hail and Farewell! Blessed be!

Pulling Up the Magick Circle

Customarily once you draw the circle, you do not leave it until you pull or take it up. After you banish the four quarters, take up the circle by following these three steps.

1. Face North with your athame in your power hand, pointed toward the North point of your magick circle. You can use the index finger of your power hand if you don't have an athame handy.

2. Slowly turn counterclockwise, and as you turn, imagine the blue-white light of the circle being drawn back into your athame. Imagine your circle vanishing.

3. Make an energetic cut across where the boundary of the circle had been, and say something like,

> The circle is open, but unbroken.
> Merry meet, merry part

And merry meet again.
Blessed be!

After you have pulled up the circle, knock three times on the altar with the base of your wand, or with the knuckles of your power hand in honor of the Triple Goddess. It is done.

★ ★ ★ Notes ★ ★ ★

$\star \star \star$ Notes $\star \star \star$

★ ★ ★ Notes ★ ★ ★

★ ★ ★ Notes ★ ★ ★

CHAPTER FIVE

Magick Spells

Each of the powerful spells in this chapter are easy to do. Step-by-step instructions plus a list of the items you will need are included in every spell. Most of the items used in these spells can be found either in this kit or around your house.

When you first start out casting spells, I would suggest that you follow the spells pretty much the way they are written. Then when you get more adept at spell casting, feel free to change them to better suit your needs and circumstances.

Also remember that spell candles are allowed to burn all the way down on their own. If you need to put them out, snuff them out with a candle-snuffer and then relight them the following day and allow them to burn down.

Thirteen-Point Wiccan Spell Checklist

Before doing any spell spinning, it is essential that you follow steps one through nine of this checklist. You must prepare your sacred space. Merely setting up an altar, lighting a candle, and saying a few words isn't going to make your magick happen. What really powers successful magick is your intention, coupled with your expectation and desire, together with the depth of your merge with the divine. The tools merely help entrain your mind to get you into a magickal state of consciousness, a state where you bridge the mortal and divine worlds.

When you are finished casting the spell, it is equally important that you follow steps eleven through thirteen. You must close your sacred space. This shows respect and thanks to the Goddess and God as well as the elemental powers. Always, and I do mean always, pull up your magick circle when you are done.

Checklist

1. Write down the spell and what benefits you expect from doing it in your Book of Shadows. Also write down the date, day of the week, moon phase, and time.

2. Gather your spell crafting tools and ingredients together and set up your altar.

3. Draw a magick circle.

4. Consecrate the water and salt.

5. Cleanse the circle.

6. Consecrate fire and air.

7. Invoke the elemental guardians.

8. Bind the circle.

9. Invite the Goddess and God into your circle.

10. Cast the spell. Keep this book handy for easy reference.

11. Write down the results of your efforts in your Book of Shadows. You may have to wait awhile to be able to do this. Also write down any other personal thoughts or feelings about the spell.

12. When your spell is completed, bid farewell to the Goddess and God and banish the four quarters.

13. Pull up the circle and put everything away.

Empowerment Spells

SMUDGING SPELL

Sage smudging wand

1. Purify your sacred space or any place by smudging. You can use the smudging wand in this kit. A candle flame works the best for lighting smudge. As soon as the wand starts to smolder, softly blow on it until it starts to smoke. I suggest that you hold the burning wand over a fireproof bowl or dish because some of the burning herbs will drop down as thick, hot ash. Also, if you are smudging indoors, be sure a fan is on and the area is well ventilated so the smudge smoke doesn't trigger your smoke alarm!

2. Now slowly walk clockwise around the area, allowing the smoke from the burning wand to waft over the entire area. Be sure to get the corners of the room. As you do this say something like,

May the Lady and Lord,
Protect and bless this space,
And rid it of any negativity.
Blessed be! So be it!

3. When you finish smudging the area or room, you can smudge yourself by allowing the smoke to flow over your body.

4. When you are done, douse the smudge wand in water to put it completely out.

Note: Smudging wands can be found at most Wiccan and health food stores or on the Internet. You can also grow or gather sage, cedar, and lavender, drying the herbs, and either tying them in sticks or using the loose dry herbs for smudging. For a smokeless alternative to smudge, use sage oil in a aromatherapy diffuser.

THE PERFECT JOB SPELL

Sage smudging wand
Tumbled quartz crystal

1. This spell should be done on the night of a New Moon. I suggest that you set up your altar in your bedroom for this spell. Follow the directions for the Smudging Spell, and smudge yourself and the crystal stone thoroughly.

2. Hold the stone in your power hand (right hand if you are right-handed). Imagine the exact kind of job you desire—the best possible job for you—something you would really enjoy doing. Speak aloud and charge the stone with your words. Ask for the kind of job you want and say when you want it. Be as specific as you can. Tell the stone your qualifications for the job and the reasons you would be the ideal person for it.

3. Take a deep breath through your mouth, and then exhale sharply through your nose. As you do this, imagine that you are charging the stone in your hand with bright white light. Your breath is the carrier wave for your desired thought. Do this three times. This is a pulsed-breath method for charging. Then chant, over and over, something like,

Crystal stone of beauty,
Bring the perfect job to me.
So be it! Blessed Be!

4. Leave the magick circle up overnight. Hold the stone in your hand as you sleep. The next morning take up the circle. Immediately afterward, make three job inquiries. When you do, be sure to have the stone with you. Hold it in your hand while talking on the phone and carry it with you when making personal contacts. Continue making three job inquiries a day until you get that perfect job.

TREE POWER SPELL

A living tree
Chalice or cup of water

1. On Full Moon Esbats or the eve of any Sabbat, go outdoors and draw your circle, being sure to include the tree in it. Walk clockwise around your circle and sprinkle it with drops of water from the chalice.

2. Stand next to the tree, and say something like,

> O great and mighty tree
> I ask for your blessing
> Empower and protect me
> As the seasons turn anew
> May you live thy life
> Young and old, strong and free
> Bright in spring, living green
> Summer rich and autumn gold
> With sturdy trunk and bough
> O swift and mighty tree
> Protect and empower me
> As I will, so shall it be!

3. Now lean against the tree and place both palms face down against the bark. Imagine the wisdom and power of the tree flowing into your palms. Close your eyes and breathe in the power of the tree for at least 5 minutes.

FAERY TWINKLING SPELL

Lavender oil
Olive oil
Small bell

1. Anoint yourself with the lavender oil. Put three drops of lavender oil from this kit into a teaspoon of olive oil (or other cooking oil). Rub a bit on both wrists, your throat, and third eye (forehead between eyebrows). Then draw a circle of bright green light over the circle you have already drawn.

2. Face the altar, pick up the bell, and ring it three times. Say something like,

Magick rings, three times three
Spells and dreams, red and green
By the powers of Earth, Air, Fire, and Sea
By the ancient powers of the faeries
Bless my life with magick. Blessed be!

Now ring the bell seven times, and then sit back.

3. Breathe rhythmically to the count of three, breathing in and counting three, holding your breath for three counts, and exhaling to the count of three. Do this three times, and then begin to imagine yourself stepping through a faery circle into an Otherworld. Begin to imagine friendly starspun faeries gathering all around you. You can see and sense their rainbow of energies empowering you. Allow the starspun faery light to completely fill you.

4. Thank the faeries and then ring the bell three times.

CANDLE MAGICK SWIFTING ENERGY SPELL

White, brown, and black candle
Dinner plate or platter
Ballpoint pen
Salt

1. Wash the candles in cool saltwater and dry them. Use the ballpoint pen to inscribe the black candle with the negative problem you want to get rid of. Then inscribe the brown candle with the word "shift." Inscribe the white candle with your positive goal—the successful result. Put the candles in a row on the plate in this order, black, brown, and white. Leave enough room between them so they don't melt each other when they are lit. Carefully pour a thick line of salt all the way around the candles in a clockwise circle.

2. Light the candles and say something like,

Circle of salt, black, brown, and white
Bring positive changes into my life
Bring them swiftly, without strife
Blessed be! So shall it be!

3. Then gaze into the candlelight and imagine the energy shifting from negative to positive. Do this for several minutes.

4. When they are done burning down, throw the candle remains and salt away in the garbage. Thoroughly clean the plate before using it again.

FORTUNE COOKIE LUCK SPELL

Miniature broom
Jar with a lid
3 pinches of thyme
3 pinches of rosemary
3 pinches of nutmeg
Fortune from a fortune cookie (one you like)

1. Use the miniature broom to sweep out the jar and lid of any unwanted energies. Next, put the herbs in the jar. Put the fortune on top of the herbs, and then firmly screw the lid on.

2. Shake the jar nine times, and then say something like,

To Goddess and God I do pray
Guide me through this day
May good fortune come my way
Make this my lucky day!
So mote it be as I say!

3. Keep the capped jar on the windowsill. For the next two weeks, each morning shake the capped jar nine times. Say the incantation, and then shake it nine more times while visualizing your magickal goal.

4. After two weeks, scatter the herbs on the ground outside your front door. Keep the fortune in a safe and appropriate place such as your wallet, purse, or a desk drawer.

POWER ANIMAL SPELL

Tumbled quartz crystal
Brown candle

1. This spell is to be done on the night of the Full Moon. Light the candle dedicating it to your favorite Goddess or God. Hold the crystal in your power hand and say this invocation three times,

Hail to my totems and power animals
On behalf of the powers of the moon
On behalf of the powers of the stars

On behalf of the Goddess and God
Hail, I invite and welcome you
Come be with me on this moonlit night!

2. Sit back comfortably, holding the stone in your receiving hand (left if you are right-handed). Gaze at the candle and begin to imagine a mysteriously shaped tree in front of you. The tree is in a magickal garden. There is a small pool with fragrant blossoms floating in the center, and you can smell the scent of the water and the flowers cradled on its surface. Breathe in deeply several times, relaxing, and feeling peaceful. Imagine you're sitting by the side of the pool and look at the flowers and their reflection upon the pool's glassy surface. As you look at the surface of the pool, you begin to see a soft shimmering light. From the center of the shimmering light, your power animal appears. You gaze at the animal's beauty for a few moments. Without fear, you move over next to it, touching it, and making contact. As you do, all of the knowledge and legacy of the power animal passes into you. Ask the animal its name. If you have any trouble discovering your power animal's name, repeat your question and wait for a response. Repeat your power animal's name over and over again to yourself. Ask your power animal a question you may have. As you remain in contact with the animal in your mind's eye, imagine that its strength and power are merging with you, energizing and boosting your personal energy and well-being. Imagine becoming one with your power animal, integrating its knowledge and power into your own being.

3. When you are done, thank your power animal for its presence and help. Clap your hands three times and thank deity.

INTERNET CHAT COMPUTER SPELL

Computer
Internet service

1. Do this spell at 9:00 P.M. on a Full Moon. When you draw your magick circle, be sure you include your computer area. Turn on your computer, sit back and merge with the menu screen for a few minutes. Take a few deep breaths to center yourself, and then go to a Wiccan chat room that you have already visited, or select a new room that you haven't been to before. There are several rooms to chose from. Please refer to my book, *The Wiccan Web* (Citadel Press, 2001), for a listing of great sites.

2. Before you enter the chat room, set the cyber stage by placing your fingertips on the keyboard, and saying something like,

O computer, cyber cauldron of creation,
Weave a Wiccan Web for my navigation.
In Internet server and user circles tonight,
Merry meet and part, may this chat be bright!
I call upon all of my Cyber friends
And invite them to click on now!
I call upon the Cyber Spirits of Earth
And invite them to click on now!
I call upon the Cyber Spirits of Air
And invite them to click on now!
I call upon the Cyber Spirits of Fire
And invite them to click on now!
I call upon the Cyber Spirits of Water
And invite them to click on now!
Blessed be all the weavers of the Web
Blessed be! Blessed be! Blessed be!

3. Enter the chat room and begin chatting.

Healing Spells

CANDLE MAGICK HEALING SPELL

Lavender oil
Olive oil
Candle
Ballpoint pen

1. This spell should be done on the night of the
Waxing Moon. Choose a candle to represent the

person to be healed. You can use a zodiac candle color or simply choose the color that you feel best represents the person. The zodiac candle colors are:

Red/Aries	Green/Taurus	Yellow/Gemini
Silver/Cancer	Orange/Leo	Blue/Virgo
Rose/Libra	Red/Scorpio	Purple/Sagittarius
Brown/Capricorn	All Colors/Aquarius	Turquoise/Pisces

2. Wash the candle in cool saltwater and dry it. Use the ballpoint pen to inscribe the person's name on the candle body three times. Put a drop of the lavender oil included in this kit into a teaspoon of olive or other cooking oil. Then dress or rub the candle body with the oil. Wipe your hands.

3. Light the candle and say something like,

Hail and welcome healing spirits
Of Earth, Air, Fire, and Water
I ask that you now come forth.
Bring strength and good health now
Earth grow, wind blow!
Fire warm, water flow!
Natural rhythms that be,
Bring healing energy to (say the person's name)!
So be it! Blessed be!

4. As you allow the candle to burn all the way down, imagine the person being strong, vital, and completely healed.

BATHING BEAUTY SPELL

Rose-colored candle
Warm bath
3 chamomile tea bags
Rose oil
A rose

1. This spell should be done during a Waxing Moon. Set up a temporary altar in the bathroom that will accommodate the candle and candlestick. Draw a sacred circle of rose-colored light. Light the candle, dedicating it to your favorite Goddess of beauty such as Venus.

2. Fill a warm bath, add the chamomile tea bags and a few drops of rose oil. Put the rose next to the tub, and then get into the bathwater.

3. Hold the rose in both hands and pull the petals off, one at a time, dropping them into the bathwater. With each petal you pull, say something like,

> Flower of loveliness and delight,
> Share your beauty with me tonight.
> As I will, make it so!

Close your eyes and think about your best features. Imagine that your best features are even better. Make them bright and shining. Continue to concentrate on your best features as you say something like,

O beautiful Lady of the night
Weaver of the elemental spirit
Bless me with your love and beauty
Beauty bright within, shining without
O Lady of the night, I pray you
Bless me with your love and beauty
Beauty bright within, shining without
So be it! So mote it be!

4. Soak for a few more minutes, and then get out of the tub and dry off. Snuff out the candle. Keep it to use when you do this spell again. Anoint yourself with the rose oil by putting a bit on each wrist and on the inside of both your ankles. Sit or lay back and imagine your beauty blossoming like a beautiful rose.

28-DAY PLACKET HEALING SPELL

3 pinches of cinnamon
3 pinches of powdered ginger
3 bay leaves
Sandalwood incense and censor
2 square 7" X 7" pieces of purple paper
Stapler
Scotch tape
Felt pen

1. This spell should be done on a Full Moon on a Sunday night. Staple and tape the two squares of paper together along the sides and bottom edge, leaving the top open. This makes the placket envelope. Use the felt pen to write the word "Heal" on both sides of the placket in large letters. Then, write the same word on both sides of each of the three bay leaves.

2. When the ink is dry, insert the three leaves into the placket opening. Add the other ingredients, and then bathe the placket in the incense smoke for a few minutes to reinforce its healing power. To charge the placket, hold it in your hands, merge with the divine, and say something like,

Energies with the power to renew,
Hear me now as I call to you.
Heal my spirit and uplift my soul,

Great Lady and Lord, pray make me whole.
Blessed dreams now heal me
As I will, so mote it be!

3. Put the placket next to your bedside or inside your pillowcase to access its healing power. Leave it there for twenty-eight nights. You can reuse the placket envelope by pouring the old herbs outside on the ground after the twenty-eight nights, and putting fresh herbs inside the placket envelope and recharging it.

CRYSTAL CASTLE HEALING SPELL

Tumbled quartz crystal
Sage smudging wand
Green candle
Healing music

1. This spell should be done on the night of a Waxing Moon. Turn on some healing music. Light the candle, dedicating it to a favorite Goddess or God of healing. Then light the smudge wand, and smudge the stone and candle for a minute or so. Or, if you prefer, you can wash the crystal and candle with cool running water. Take a few moments to center your mind.

2. Hold the stone in your hands. Gaze at the

stone and merge with it. As you do this, say
something like,

> Stone of healing, stone of might
> Heal me with your light tonight
> Stone of power, from this hour
> Bring to me the healing I seek
> As I now will, so mote it be!

3. Breathe deeply three times, and continue
merging with the stone. Begin to imagine a beautiful castle within the crystal's center. Now close
your eyes. Imagine entering the castle within the
stone. Allow all of your senses to come alive as
you see, touch, smell, hear, and even taste your
surroundings. With each deep breath you take,
you find yourself in another fascinating room in
your castle. As you take another deep breath, you
suddenly find yourself in a large room, much
larger than any of the others, with a magnificent
healing spring spilling out of the floor in the center of the room, and into a immense pool made of
solid crystal. Imagine moving over to the spring,
and shedding your clothes. You sit or lay back
in the spring, noticing how warm and silky the
crystal-clear water feels as it flows over your skin.
Allow the soft bubbling water of the thermal
spring to absorb all of your pain, hurt, illness, or
disease. Release your pain into the healing waters. Keep doing this until you feel a sense of
relief. Then imagine the warm healing water

flowing over your entire being for a few minutes and completely recharging your energy.

4. When you are done, be sure to keep the crystal on your altar, using it whenever you want to experience the healing waters of the castle spring. In the next week, try to spend some time by a lake, river, the ocean, or sit by a fountain. Imagine the healing powers of the water flowing into you.

GOOD HEALTH SPELL

A candle to represent yourself (select your
own color)
A black candle, blue candle, orange candle, and
white candle

1. Wash the candles in cool saltwater and dry them. Inscribe your initials, name, or magickal name on the candle that represents you.

2. Before you light the candles, face the altar and say something like,

I call upon the powers of the Goddess this night.
I call upon the powers of the God this night.
I call upon the ancient powers that be.
Sacred candles, sacred light, aid the magick that
I name.

I seek good health and positive change on this
fortunate night.

3. Light the candle representing yourself and
say something like,

This is me (say your full name or
magickal name),
This is everything that I am.

Light the black candle and say something like,

This is my poor health. Leave!
I banish my illness and bid it farewell,
Now and forevermore!

Light the blue candle and say something like,

This washes away my poor health,
Now and forevermore!

Light the orange candle and say something like,

This represents the healing energy and
good health
That are coming my way right now.
I welcome these divine blessings with
open arms.

Light the white candle and say something like,

This is divine power that I need to make it so.
So be it! Blessed be!

4. Gaze at the candles for several minutes while chanting something like,

> I welcome healing. I welcome good health.
> So be it! Blessed be!

5. Allow the candles to burn completely down to carry your wishes into the universe.

SLEEP MAGICK SPELL

Small bowl of sand
3 small pebbles
Soothing music

1. Turn on soft music and dim the lights. Use your fingers to create a hole in the middle of the bowl of sand. Slowly sift the sand with your fingers while thinking about the things in your life that are troubling you right now. Imagine putting all of your troubles into the hole in the sand. Try to actually feel yourself energetically tossing them into the bowl of sand.

2. Cover the hole over and level out the sand, placing the three pebbles on its surface. As you do this, say something like,

> Peaceful sands of sleep, troubles buried so deep
> The Sand Man sings, sleep a while, sleep a while.
> Peaceful sea of dreams, worries washed away

The Sand Man sings, sleep a while, sleep a while.
As I so will, so mote it be! Blessed be!

Put the bowl back on your altar.

3. Lay back in bed and imagine yourself on a sandy beach on a warm evening. Imagine digging a deep hole in the soft, warm sand. You can feel the warmth of the sand on your fingers, hands, and arms as you dig, and you can smell the salt in the air, water, and earth. All of these sensations help you feel more and more relaxed and peaceful. The hole you have been digging is now deep enough. You begin to energetically pour all your problems and worries into the hole, letting go of them.

4. Once all of your problems and worries are in the hole, imagine using your hands to fill it in. Imagine patting the sand down on the top of the hole, and placing three small pebbles on its surface.

5. Now imagine yourself laying back on the warm sand. Slowly allow the evening sun and rhythmic surf to lull you to sleep, feeling peaceful and calm, warm and sleepy.

6. Keep the three pebbles on your altar to remind you of your natural ability to let go of problems. Bury the sand in a hole outside.

SWEET DREAMS SPELL

Pair of shoes
Lavender oil

1. This spell should be done on the night of a New Moon. Anoint yourself with the lavender oil, applying a drop to the top of your head, inside both wrists, and on the bottom of your feet. As you do, say something like,

> As I now dream and sleep
> Nightmares can no longer plague me,
> Help me divine and ancient Ones,
> Protect me now and forevermore!
> So be it! Ayea! Ayea! Ayea!

2. Put a drop of the oil inside each of the shoes, and place them next to your bed, pointing them toward the door. Then slide into bed backwards, and sit or lay back comfortably. Stare at your hands—and *only* your hands—for at least fifteen minutes. Focus all of your attention on them.

3. After focusing on your hands, close your eyes, and take a few deep breaths. Then open your eyes, and clap your hands three times. Say three times,

> Hands help me, hands wake me.
> As I will, so shall it be!

4. As you lay back to sleep, cross your hands over your chest or stomach. Close your eyes and imagine your hands in your mind's eye, and keep imagining them until you fall asleep. If you find yourself in an unpleasant dream, all you have to do is simply imagine your hands, and you will immediately wake up.

Love Spells

HOW DO I LOVE THEE SPELL

Miniature broom
Lavender oil
Pentacle
Red candle
Olive oil

1. Wash the candle in cool saltwater and dry it. Inscribe the candle with the words "I love thee" and your lover's or intended lover's initials. Inscribe your initials on top of your lover's. Then put a drop of lavender oil in a teaspoon of olive or other cooking oil, and rub it on the candle. When you are finished, set the candle in the candlestick on the altar. Anoint yourself with the lavender oil, and then wipe your hands.

2. Next, gently sweep your altar with your miniature broom with the intention of sweeping out all negativity, loneliness, doubt, and fear. Set the broom on the left side of your altar surface.

3. Light the candle, dedicating it to your favorite love Goddess. Merge with the flame, with the Fire element, and hold the pentacle in your hand. Charge the pentacle by saying something like,

By thy power Mother Goddess, by Earth, Air, Fire, and Sea
Pray bring my love to me, by thy power Great Lady
I will love thee to the depth my soul can reach.
I will love thee by Moon, Sun, and candlelight.
I will love thee freely, I love thee purely,
I will love thee with passion and compassion
I will love thee with the breath and smiles of all my life
By thy power Mother Goddess, by Earth, Air, Fire, and Sea
Pray bring my mate to me, by thy power Great Lady
As I will, so shall it be! Blessed be!

Set the pentacle at the center of the altar.

4. Pick up your miniature broom, and once again, gently sweep the altar, only this time, imagine you are sweeping *in* love, romance, passion, and joy into your life right now. Do this for a minute or so. Allow the candle to burn down on its own.

Carry the pentacle on your person to attract your mate.

DANDELION LOVE SPELL

A dandelion

1. On the night of the Full Moon, invoke the elemental guardians and draw a magick circle first. Then pick a dandelion puffball.

2. Hold the dandelion in your hands and make an affirming love wish. For example, a new lover, a happier relationship, a more understanding partner, or a little spice in your love life. As you hold the dandelion, focus on your wish and say something like,

> Help me Goddess, with all your might
> I wish upon this moon ball tonight
> Please take this token of my love
> As your silver light shines from above
> May my wish fly swiftly unto me
> As I wish, so shall it be!

3. Blow on the dandelion until it is completely gone, letting the wind take your wish.

4. Thank the Goddess.

ROSE LOVE WISH SPELL

Rose bush
Red ribbon
Small piece of paper
Red pen

1. Use the pen to write the one love wish that is most important to you. Roll the paper into a small scroll. Hold the scroll in your hands and empower it by saying something like,

> Joy be free, joy to chose
> By rain and winds come loose
> May my wish come to me.
> Blessed be! So mote it be!

2. Loosely tie the scroll with the ribbon to the rose bush.

3. With the wind and rain, your wish is liberated from the rose bush and is free to come true.

STUCK ON YOU LOVE SPELL

Vanilla oil
3 sticks of cinnamon gum
3 pinches of cinnamon
3 almonds
Vanilla incense
Red candle
Ballpoint pen
Red sock or pouch (which cannot be reused)
Red ribbon

1. This spell should be done during a Full Moon. Wash the candle in cool saltwater and dry it. Use the ballpoint pen to inscribe your initials and your lover's initials on the candle body. Draw a clockwise circle around the initials. Dress the candle with vanilla oil. Also anoint yourself. You can easily make your own instant vanilla oil by putting a few drops of pure vanilla in a teaspoon of olive oil. I like to put a vanilla bean in a bottle of carrier oil like apricot oil, let it set for an entire moon cycle, and then use it for spells like this one. When you are done dressing the candle, set it in the candlestick upon the altar, and wipe the oil off your hands.

2. Light the candle, dedicating it to your favorite love Goddess. Then light the incense, using the candle flame, dedicating it to your favorite love God this time.

3. Put the pinches of cinnamon, almonds, and three drops of vanilla oil into the sock. Bathe the sock and the gum pieces in the incense for a minute or two. Then chew the sticks of gum, one at a time, and put the chewed pieces into the sock. Anoint the sock with vanilla oil. Hold the sock in your hands, gaze at the candle flame, merge with the Goddess and God, and say something like,

Great Goddess, Mother of us all
I summon you Lady of the Moon
And invite your loving power into this circle
May you bring me and my love closer together
Great God, Father of us all
I summon you Lord of the forests
And invite your loving power into this circle
May you bring me and my love closer together
I ask this in the Lady and Lord's names (say
their names)
As I ask, so shall it be! Blessed be!

4. Continue speaking directly to the Goddess and God. Pour out your heart to them. Explain the reasons you want to be closer to the one you love right now. Ask for their help and blessings. The more intensely you do this, the stronger the results of the spell.

5. When the candle has completely burned down, put the remaining wax in the sock. Tie the sock with the ribbon. Put it under your bed or somewhere else that is secret and safe.

VALENTINE'S DAY SPELL

9 bay leaves (preferably fresh)
Warm bath

1. Do this spell on the eve of Valentine's Day. Take four bay leaves, tear or crush them, and put the leaves in a cup of boiling water. Let them soak in the water for about 15 minutes, and then strain the leaves out, and pour the water into a warm bath.

2. Dim the lights, close your eyes, and relax in the bay bath for about 10 minutes. Imagine your true love coming into your life. If your mind wanders, just bring your focus back to imagining your true love. Be creative and have fun!

3. Get out of the tub and dry off. Take the remaining bay leaves and put one in each corner of your pillowcase, and the fifth leaf under your pillow. Get into bed and as you drift to sleep, silently repeat these words:

Blessed bay spirit, bring my true love to me.

4. Done properly, this spell will inspire dreams of the person you are destined to fall in love with.

JUNE MOON LOVE SPELL

Lavender oil
White candle
Ballpoint pen
Silver pin
Photo of your love
Soft music

1. Do this spell on a Full Moon in June. Wash the candle in cool saltwater, dry it, and put it on the altar. Inscribe the candle three times with the word "Love." Turn on some soft music. Then inscribe your initials and your lover's initials on the candle. Encircle the initials together with a circle or heart. Next, dress the candle with lavender oil and put it in its holder upon the altar. Anoint yourself with the oil and wipe your hands.

2. Put the photo in front of the candle. Take the silver needle and pierce the wick of the unlit candle. Light the candle, merge with the flame, and say something like,

> Sacred flame of the high moon,
> Fill me with love and make me swoon.
> Sacred light, burn strong and bright,
> Bring to me my soul's delight.
> For the good of all and harm to none
> Blessed be! This spell is done!

3. Don't take up the circle until the next day. Allow the candle to safely burn all the way down. As you drift to sleep, visualize making love under the Full Moon.

4. When you awaken, pull up the circle. Then take the silver needle and fasten it to the right top corner of the photo. Place the photo with pin under or next to your bed.

THREE FATES STRING MAGICK

3 pieces of string (each about 12 inches long)
A white candle
An uplifting love song

1. This spell should be done during a Full Moon. Wash the candle in cool saltwater and dry it. Put the candle on the altar and turn on the music. Light the candle, dedicating it to the three Fates or the Norns—Urd, Verdandi, and Skuld.

2. Sit or stand before your altar for a few minutes, gazing at the candle flame, and temporarily letting go of all your worries. Calm your mind as much as you can.

3. Take the three pieces of string and braid them together, knotting both ends. As you tie each knot, say something like,

Weaving destiny's web tonight
By the warm candlelight,
Bring my lover on this night.
Threads of the Fates,
Open the bright starry gate,
And bring me my moon mate.
So be it! So mote it be!

Keep knotting the braid, over and over again, until you can't knot it again. Each time you tie a knot, repeat the incantation. Focus all of your attention on your task, on bringing your moon mate to you. Allow your fingers, your hands, and the string to tell the story of what you truly desire, knotting your desire into the string and bringing it into your life. Merge completely and imagine tying into this radiant energy, threading this light and love into your life. Feel the movement of your fingers, hands, and thread becoming one with your intention, expectation, desire, and joined in light.

4. When you are finished, put the knotted string under your pillow while you sleep. Leave the circle drawn overnight.

5. In the morning, pull up the circle. Take the string outside and bury it beneath a favorite flower bush. This encourages your moon mate's love to grow and blossom.

PENTACLE LOVE CHARM

Sage smudge wand
Red candle
Piece of paper
Pen

1. Smudge the pentacle, candle, paper, and pen.

2. Light the candle, dedicating it to a favorite love Goddess.

3. On the sheet of paper, draw an original symbol of love on the paper. Do this by merging with the divine, and then just drawing whatever comes to you. You can use symbols you are familiar with, such as the heart or circle, even connecting them together into one big symbol. Write your lover's initials and your initials across your original symbol. Then draw a pentacle on top of your initials.

4. Fold the paper in half, and then in half again, and once more. Seal it with wax from the candle. Do this carefully so you don't burn or spill wax on yourself or the furnishings. It takes a little practice to get a good seal with the wax.

5. Now hold the charm in your power hand, and say something like,

More loving, more caring,
More joy, more sharing.
So be it! Blessed be!

6. Place the charm among your lover's belongings, for example, in a coat pocket in the closet.

BRIDGET'S DAY FERTILITY SPELL

Miniature broom
A sheet of green paper
A green felt pen
A green ribbon
Fresh flowers in a vase filled with water
A green stone
6 handfuls of rich soil in a bowl
A fruit-bearing tree

1. Cast this spell on the eve of Bridget's Day (Imbolc) in your bedroom. Use the miniature broom to gently sweep your altar clean of any unwanted energies. As you do this, say,

May all evil and foulness be gone
I ask this in our Lady Bridget's name
Sacred Goddess of home and hearth
Bless and protect me tonight!

Set the broom on the left side of your altar when you are done sweeping.

2. Use the green felt pen to write the exact results you expect from this spell. For example, "I (name) and my lover (name) want to conceive a strong, bright, healthy boy child in the next year." Take a handful of the soil and put it on the paper. Then put the green stone on top of the soil. Then fold the soil and stone up in the paper, folding the paper a total of three times. Wind the ribbon around the folded paper three times and then knot it tight with three knots. Hold the paper in your hands, and say,

> Bright Goddess of jeweled starlight
> Generous mother of the Earth
> Swift sister of the four winds
> You who kindle the creative fire
> Passionate lover of the sea
> Make us fertile and help us conceive
> The healthy and happy child of our dreams.
> Soil of fertility, stone of birth,
> Divine powers of Air, Fire, Water and Earth,
> Make us fertile and help us conceive
> The bright and strong child of our dreams.
> So be it! So mote it be! Blessed be!

3. Place the paper and bowl of soil on the altar, and leave the magick circle up overnight. As you drift to sleep, repeat the words, "Fertility grow, make it so!"

4. In the morning, pull up the circle. Take the paper and bowl of soil outdoors. Bury the folded paper under the eastern-most base of a fruit-bearing tree. Then divide the soil in the bowl into three equal handfuls and toss them gently around the base of the tree, moving clockwise. With each handful you toss, say,

> Sacred tree help us conceive
> The healthy child of our dreams.
> As I will, so shall it be!

Thank the tree spirit.

5. Keep the fresh flowers next to your bedside to increase fertility. When they wither, place them under the same fruit tree, and say,

> Fertile flowers and sacred tree
> Help us conceive the child of our dreams.

6. Over the next year, tend to the tree, touching, watering, and caring for it as you would a beloved child.

DREAM LOVER SPELL

A red rose
Red candle
Ballpoint pen
Rose oil
A red sock

1. This spell should be done on the night of a Waxing Moon. Wash the candle in cool saltwater and dry it. Inscribe the candle with the words "Dream Lover." Then rub a few drops of rose oil on the candle, your wrists, ankles, throat, and forehead. Wipe the oil from your hands, and light the candle.

2. Clear your mind, take a few deep breaths, and then take the rose and hold it gently between your hands. Smell it, taking a few more deep breaths as you inhale its fragrance. Now hold the rose in front of the candle, so that it is illuminated, and say something like,

Candle light, sacred light,
Burn steady, burn bright.
Scent of rose, fill the night.
Dream lover, I do invite.
With this rose as my gift,
Soft asleep I do drift.
In my dreams, make us one,
So be it, this charm is done!

Comfortably recline and gaze at the candle flame. As the candle burns down, imagine the perfect dream lover.

3. Leave the magick circle in place overnight and put the rose by your bed. As you drift to sleep, silently repeat over and over,

Dream lover come to me.

4. In the morning, pull up the circle. Then remove the stem of the rose, and return it to the Earth. Put the rose petals inside the red sock. Keep the sock inside your pillowcase for the next month to draw your dream lover to you.

SOULMATE MAGICK SPELL

A sheet of paper and pen
White candle
Vanilla oil
Tumbled crystal

1. On the piece of paper, write down all of the qualities you want in a soulmate. Place the paper on your altar where you can see it.

2. Wash the candle in cool saltwater and dry it. Inscribe the word "Soulmate" on the candle. Dress it with the vanilla oil, all the while imagining your soulmate. Place the candle in its holder and light it. While staring into the flame, see each one of the characteristics of your soulmate coming to life in the fire. Say these words,

> Who is my soulmate?
> Show my soulmate to me,
> In this fire, in this flame
> In this life. So mote it be!

3. Now take the crystal from the altar. Rub it with vanilla oil. Hold it in your receiving hand (left if you are right-handed), and repeat,

> Who is my soulmate?
> Show my soulmate to me,
> In this fire, in this flame,
> In this life. So mote it be!

4. Imagine yourself entering into the flame as if it is a doorway into another dimension. There are images before you that start to come into focus. You see the image of your soulmate before you. Continue doing this as the candle burns down.

FLOWER POWER LOVE SPELL

A package of flower seeds
A green candle

1. Light the candle, dedicating it to a Goddess of abundance such as Fortuna. Put the seed packet in front of the candle, and imagine planting the seeds. Imagine yourself watering and cultivating them. In your mind's eye, watch the flowers grow strong and beautiful.

2. Next, hold the seed packet up in your hands, and charge it by saying something like,

Flower seeds, bring me love power
Growing stronger with each passing hour
Bring passion and joy and let it grow
As I will, it shall be so!

Hold the seeds between your hands until the packet feels warm to the touch.

3. Put the packet back upon your altar in front of the candle. Imagine the flowers blooming and thriving. Chant these words over and over,

Seeds of passion
Bring me love
And let it grow
As I will, make it so!

4. The next day, plant the seeds in the proper location, depending upon the type of flower. As you do this, merge with the elements of Earth, Air, Fire, Water, and spirit. Water the seeds regularly, tend to the seedlings, and watch them grow. As they grow, so too, does the love in your life.

SHAKESPEARE IN LOVE CANDLE MAGICK

Red candle
Ballpoint pen
Lavender oil

1. Wash the candle in cool saltwater, dry it, and then place it in its holder on your altar. Inscribe the candle with the word "Love." Dress it with lavender oil. Also anoint your forehead, both wrists, and ankles. Wipe the oil from your hands.

2. Light the candle, merge with the powers of Fire, and slowly read William Shakespeare's Sonnet 18 aloud:

Shall I compare thee to a summer's day?
Thou art more lovely and more temperate.
Rough winds do shake the darling buds of May,
And summer's lease hath all too short a date.
Sometime too hot the eye of heaven shines,
And often is his gold complexion dimmed,
And every fair from fair sometime declines,

By chance or nature's changing course
untrimmed.
But thy eternal summer shall not fade,
Nor lose possession of that fair thou owest,
Nor shall Death brag thou wander'st in
his shade
When in eternal lines to time thou grow'st.
So long as men can breathe, or eyes can see,
So long lives this, and this gives life to thee.

3. Gaze at the candle flame as the candle burns down. Imagine true love coming into your life. See the pictures in your head and feel the feelings of being truly and passionately loved.

Prosperity Spells

CANDLE MAGICK PROSPERITY SPELL

A green pillar candle
Cinnamon oil

1. Begin this spell on a Sunday night, preferably just about a week before the Full Moon. Wash the candle in cool saltwater and dry it.

2. Inscribe the candle body with your name and words such as *prosperity, abundance, wealth, money, riches, fortune, plenty*. Dress the candle with cinnamon oil. Make your own cinnamon oil by putting a pinch of ground cinnamon in a tea-spoon of olive, sesame, or other cooking oil, and mixing it together. To empower the candle, hold it firmly in both hands until you feel it heat up slightly. Set the candle on the altar and wipe your hands.

3. Light the candle and as you do, say something like,

> By the divine light of the Goddess and God
> This candle shall bring me prosperity, fortune, and wealth.
> By my will, so shall it be! Blessed be!

Gaze at the candle flame and as you do begin imagining prosperity, wealth, and riches coming into your life. Try on the picture in your mind, the feelings of abundance and plenty. Do this for at least 15 minutes. When you are done, snuff out the candle.

4. Each night for a week, relight the candle, repeat the spell, and visualization. On the seventh night, allow the candle to burn all the way down.

MONEY ON TREES SPELL

A fruit-bearing tree
A dollar bill
A green ribbon
Sage smudging wand
A pinch of cinnamon
A pinch of rosemary
A green sock

1. Bathe the sock and dollar bill in the smudge smoke for a couple of minutes. Then open the sock and put the herbs in it. Fold the dollar bill eight times and put it in the sock too. Tie the sock closed with the ribbon, knotting the ribbon eight times.

2. To charge the money sock, hold it in your hands, and say three times,

Money sock of green
Bring the fruits of abundance to me
May my wealth grow like this tree
Bring the fruits of joy and prosperity
May my abundance grow like this tree
By Earth, Air, Fire, and Sea
So be it! So shall it be!

3. As you watch the candle burn down, imagine experiencing lasting prosperity. Let your imagination run wild!

4. Tie the sock onto a fruit-bearing tree so your wealth will grow as it grows.

GOOD BUSINESS SPELL

A bowl of crushed sweet basil leaves

1. Hold the bowl of crushed herbs upward toward your altar. Merge with the Goddess and God, and say something like,

Great Goddess, I ask you to join me tonight
I pray you, assist me in my rite
Guide, protect, and help me in my business
Bring those who are bright and repel those
who harm
Great God, I ask you to join me tonight
I pray you, assist me in my rite
Guide, protect, and help me in my business
Bring those who are bright and repel those
who harm
As I will, so shall it be!

2. Sprinkle the basil around the main entrance of your place of business. As you do this, chant the names of your favorite goddesses and gods.

SILVER-GREEN MONEY MAGNET

Sage smudging wand
Silver coin
Green doormat
Small magnet

1. Smudge the coin, doormat, and magnet to clear them of any unwanted energies.

2. Put the doormat in front of the main entrance of your home.

3. Hold the coin and magnet in your power hand. Merge with the Goddess and God, and say,

North, East, South, and West
By the Goddess, I am divinely blessed
Bring great riches to my doorstep
From the North, East, South, and West
By the God, I am divinely blessed
Bring me prosperity and success
As I will, so mote it be!

4. Now put the coin and magnet under the doormat, and leave them there to attract riches and success. Recharge the coin and magnet every month to bring more prosperity into your life.

PENTACLE MONEY SPELL

Pentacle
Sandalwood incense

1. Do this spell in your bedroom on the night of a Waxing Moon. Light the incense, dedicating it to a favorite Goddess of prosperity. Bathe the pentacle in the incense smoke for a minute or two.

2. Hold the pentacle in your hand and imagine a bright green light filling it. Begin to imagine the pentacle expanding. As you do this, also imagine your wealth expanding. Keep your mind focused on seeing and feeling your wealth expanding. Imagine having all the money you need. Really feel what that feels like. Put that feeling into the pentacle.

3. Hold the pentacle in your receiving hand. Leave the circle down as you drift to sleep, repeat silently,

Magick pentacle bring to me,
Enriching dreams of prosperity.

4. In the morning, write down everything you remember from your dreams. Pull up your magick circle, and put the pentacle on your altar. At night, hold it in your left hand as you drift to sleep. The more you repeat this spell, the more dream messages you will receive on how to make more money.

GREEN UNDERWEAR MONEY SPELL

A pair of green colored underwear
Green candle
Ballpoint pen

1. Put on the pair of green underwear. The underwear represents the "Wearing of the Green," a Celtic tradition in honor of Earth's new green garment in spring.

2. Inscribe the candle with three dollar signs. Put the candle on the altar and light it. Focus on the center of the flame, and begin to see a prosperous new you. As you do this, repeat the following nine times,

Wearing green, sight unseen,
Bring me wealth as I dream.
As I will, so shall it be!

3. Continue gazing at the candle as it burns down and imagine having plenty of money. Know that each time you wear your lucky green underwear, you will find more money in your pocket.

CANDLE MAGICK ABUNDANCE SPELL

Green candle
Pen
Patchouli oil
8 pinches of sesame seeds

1. Do this spell on the night of a Waxing Moon. Wash the candle in cool saltwater and dry it. Inscribe the name of your favorite Goddess of abundance on the candle. Inscribe your name next to hers. Join the names together with a large dollar sign, and then inscribe a circle around the names and symbol. Rub a thin film of patchouli oil on the candle body and put it in its holder on the altar. Use the oil on your hands to anoint the top of your head, your forehead, and the bottoms of your feet. Wipe the oil from your hands and then sprinkle the sesame seeds around the candlestick in a clockwise circle.

2. Light the candle, dedicating it to the Goddess, while saying something like,

Candle of abundance and plenty,
Let your fire flame fill me.
By the will of (name of the Goddess).
With leaps that generously abound,
My money grows all year round.
So be it! So mote it be!

3. As the candle burns down, imagine being surrounded by and filled with a brilliant, warm green light.

SILVER COIN LUCKY CHARM

Silver coin
Silver candle
Sage smudging wand
Bowl of water

1. Do this spell on a night of the Full Moon. Put the bowl of water in the middle of your altar. Place the candle and candlestick behind the bowl. Smudge the coin.

2. Light the candle, dedicating it to a favorite moon Goddess of prosperity. Ask her to offer her blessings and power to your charm. Now hold the coin, and charge it by saying something like,

Silver coin, silver moon
Bring me luck, bring it soon
Lucky coin, fortunate moon
Bring me wealth, bring it soon
As I will, so shall it be!

3. Drop the coin into the bowl of water. Gaze into the water, observing how the candlelight plays upon its surface and the surface of the coin. Do this for at least 15 minutes. Then take a few minutes to imagine both your luck and wealth growing. Delight in your abundance.

4. Take the coin out of the water and put it in your pocket, wallet, or purse. Pour the water from the bowl into the ground just outside your front door to attract even more luck and wealth.

Protection Spells

CRYSTAL PROTECTION TALISMAN

Tumbled quartz crystal
Sage smudging wand

1. Do this spell on the night of a Waxing Moon. Smudge the crystal stone.

2. Hold the stone in your power hand and face your altar. Merge with the divine, using your emotions, sensation, or whatever works for you, and fill your mind with a bright white light, edged in cobalt blue. Put that light into the stone. Actually imagine the light being absorbed into the atomic structure of the stone. To charge the stone, hold it in your power hand, and say,

Stone of protection, crystal stone of power
Whisperers of the night, I pray you
May the road rise up to meet me
May the wind be always at my back
May the sun shine warm on my face
May the rain fall soft upon my home
May the Goddess bless and protect me
May the God bless and protect me
As I will it, so shall it be!

3. Continue holding the stone, and imagine its area of influence. Do this by actually visualizing a bright field of white and cobalt blue light surrounding it, and shooting out about ten feet in all directions from it. See and sense the stone's field of influence a total of three times to set it in place.

4. After completing these steps, put your talisman on your altar for a moment, and clap your hands loudly three times. Afterward, carry your talisman in your purse or pants pocket for protection.

BROOM SWEEPING SPELL

Miniature broom

1. Stand facing your altar. Use the miniature broom to sweep the altar, moving clockwise, sweep from the center outward. With each sweeping motion, imagine the altar being washed energetically with a cobalt blue light, while saying something like,

> Sweep out evil, sweep out ill,
> Where I do the Lady's will.
> Besom, besom, Lady's broom
> Sweep out darkness, sweep out doom.
> So be it! Blessed be!

2. Now sweep the altar once more, this time imagine sweeping away all of your problems. Feel your worries all being swept away.

HAPPY HOME SPELL

A white candle
A feather
A chalice or cup of water
A bowl filled with 6 pinches of crushed rosemary

1. Light the candle, dedicating it to your favorite Goddess or God.

2. Hold the feather in your power hand. Face East and wave the feather three times, side-to-side. Merge with the powers of Air, and say,

Powers of the East, masters of Air
I greet, honor, and welcome you here!
Powers of the East, masters of the four winds
Bring happiness to my home and be my friend!

Set the feather back upon the altar.

3. Hold the candlestick with the lit candle up and face South. Wave the candle from side-to-side three times, being careful of dripping wax. Merge with powers of Fire, and say,

Powers of the South, masters of Fire
I greet, honor, and welcome you here!
Powers of the South, masters of light
Bring happiness to my home and
blessings bright!

Set the candle upon the altar.

4. Hold the chalice in your hands. Face West, dip your fingers into the water, and sprinkle the West quarter. Do this three times, while merging with the powers of Water, and say,

Powers of the West, masters of Water
I greet, honor, and welcome you here!
Powers of the West, masters of fin and fish

Bring happiness to my home and grant my wish!

Set the chalice upon the altar.

5. Hold the bowl of herbs in your hands. Face North, and sprinkle three pinches of the herbs onto the floor. Merge with the powers of Earth, and say,

> Powers of the North, masters of Earth
> I greet, honor, and welcome you here!
> Powers of the North, masters of the sacred land
> Bring happiness to my home and lend a
> helping hand!

Place the bowl back on the altar.

6. Facing your altar, hold your arms upward. Merge with Oneness, and say,

> Helpful powers of Earth, Air, Fire, and Water
> I greet, honor, and welcome you here!
> Bring happiness to my home
> So be it! Blessed be!

7. Take the bowl of herbs and scatter tiny bits throughout the corners of your home. Start just inside your front door, and move clockwise. Cover the four corners of each room with a tiny sprinkle.

8. When you are done, gaze at the candle flame on the altar for a few minutes. Imagine the candle flame being a bright spirit light.

9. Close your eyes, and begin to see and feel the white spirit light growing larger and filling you and your home with happy, joyful, and loving energy.

PET PROTECTION SPELL

Your pet
Venus water

1. Do this spell on the night of the Full Moon. You can sit with your pet outside under the moon, or you can sit indoors where you can see the moon outside. Talk with your pet and praise him or her. Tell your animal friend how much you care for him or her. Most of us have little nicknames and words of endearment we say to our pets. Do so, and as you do this, imagine a protective sphere of bright white light surrounding your pet.

2. Sprinkle your pet with Venus water. Rub the water into the animal's fur or skin. As you do this, merge with your pet, and say this protective blessing,

I call upon the Moon Goddess and Horned God,
I call upon the starspun powers of Oneness,
I call upon all of the living creatures of the Earth.
By Earth, Air, Fire, and Sea, by divine will,
I ask that you work this protective spell,
Please guard (say name of pet) while sleeping
and waking,
And protect this animal from all negativity
and harm.
In all worlds, in all times! So be it! Make it so!

Tell your pet how much you love him or her, and then let your pet go. Clap your hands three times.

3. Every day, to reinforce the protective energy of this spell, take a few minutes and imagine your pet being surrounded with a protective sphere of divine white light.

★ ★ ★ NOTES ★ ★ ★

★ ★ ★ NOTES ★ ★ ★

★ ★ ★ NOTES ★ ★ ★

SUGGESTED READING

Alexander, Skye. *Magickal Astrology.* Franklin Lakes, N.J.: New Page Books, 2000.

Andrews, Ted. *Animal Speak.* St. Paul, Minn.: Llewellyn Publications, 1993.

Bowes, Susan. *Notions and Potions.* New York: Sterling Publishing Co., Inc., 1997.

Cunningham, Scott. *The Complete Book of Incense, Oils, and Brews.* St. Paul, Minn.: Llewellyn Publications, 1989.

————. *Encyclopedia of Magical Herbs.* St. Paul, Minn.: Llewellyn Publications, 1985.

————. *Living Wicca.* St. Paul, Minn.: Llewellyn Publications, 1993.

Currot, Phyllis. *Book of Shadows.* New York: Broadway Books, 1998.

————. *WitchCrafting.* New York: Broadway Books, 2001.

Drew, A. J. *Wicca for Men.* New York: Citadel Press, 1998.

—————. *Wicca Spell Crafting for Men.* Franklin Lakes, N.J.: New Page Books, 2001.

Farrar, Janet and Stewart. *The Witches' Way.* London: Robert Hale, 1984.

—————. *A Witches' Bible Compleat.* New York: Magical Childe, 1984.

Farrar, Stewart, *What Witches Do.* London: Peter Davis Limited, 1971.

Ford, Patrick K., trans. *The Mabinogi and Other Medieval Welsh Tales.* Los Angeles: University of California Press, 1977.

Gimbutas, Marija. *The Language of the Goddess.* San Francisco: Harper & Row, 1989.

Godwin, Malcolm. *The Lucid Dreamer.* New York: Simon & Schuster, 1994.

Grimassi, Raven. *The Wiccan Mysteries.* St. Paul, Minn.: Llewellyn Publications, 1997.

Hopman, Ellen Evert. *A Druid's Herbal for the Sacred Earth Year.* Rochester, N.Y.: Destiny Books, 1995.

Knight, Sirona. *A Witch Like Me.* Franklin Lakes, N.J.: New Page Books, 2001.

—————. *Celtic Traditions.* New York: Citadel Press, 2000.

—————. *Dream Magic: Night Spells and Rituals for Love, Prosperity, and Personal Power.* San Francisco: HarperSanFrancisco, 2000.

—————. *Exploring Celtic Druidism.* Franklin Lakes, N.J.: New Page Books, 2001.

—————. *Love, Sex, and Magick.* New York: Citadel Press, 1999.

—————. *Moonflower: Erotic Dreaming With the Goddess.* St. Paul, Minn.: Llewellyn Publications, 1996.

————. *The Pocket Guide to Celtic Spirituality*. Freedom, CA.: Crossing Press, 1998.

————. *The Pocket Guide to Crystals and Gemstones*. Freedom, CA.: Crossing Press, 1998.

————, et al. *The Shapeshifter Tarot*. St. Paul, Minn.: Llewellyn Publications, 1998.

————. *The Witch and Wizard Training Guide*. New York: Citadel Press, 2001.

Knight, Sirona, and Patricia Telesco. *The Wiccan Web*. New York: Citadel Press, 2001.

Leach, Maria, ed. *Standard Dictionary of Folklore, Mythology, and Legend*. N.Y.: Funk & Wagnalls Co., 1950.

Melville, Francis. *Love Potions and Charms*. Hauppauge, N.Y.: Barron's, 2001.

Monaghan, Patricia. *The Book of Goddesses and Heroines*. St. Paul, Minn.: Llewellyn Publications, 1990.

Morrison, Dorothy. *Everyday Magic*. St Paul, Minn.: Llewellyn Publications, 1998.

Sabrina, Lady. *The Witch's Master Grimoire*. Franklin Lakes, N.J.: New Page Books, 2001.

————. *Exploring Wicca*. Franklin Lakes, N.J.: New Page Books, 2000.

Starhawk. *The Spiral Dance*. San Francisco: Harper-SanFrancisco, 1979.

Stewart, R .J. *Celtic Gods, Celtic Goddesses*. New York: Sterling Publishing Co., 1990.

————. *The Power Within the Land*. Rockport, Mass.: Element Books, 1992.

Telesco, Patricia. *A Charmed Life*. Franklin Lakes, N.J.: New Page Books, 2000.

————. *Exploring Candle Magick*. Franklin Lakes, N.J.: New Page Books, 2000.

————. *Spinning Spells, Weaving Wonders*. Freedom, CA.: Crossing Press, Inc., 1996.

————. *A Witch's Beverages and Brews*. Franklin Lakes, N.J.: New Page Books, 2001.

Tuitean, Paul, and Estelle Daniels. *Pocket Guide to Wicca*. Freedom, Cal.: Crossing Press, 1998.

Valiente, Doreen. *Witchcraft for Tomorrow*. New York: St. Martin's Press, 1978.

Weinstein, Marion. *Earth Magic*. New York: Earth Magic Productions, 1998.

Williams, David, and Kate West. *Born in Albion*. Cheshire, England: Pagan Media, Ltd., 1996.

Worwood, Valerie. *The Complete Book of Essential Oils and Aromatherapy*. New York: New World Library, 1995.

ABOUT THE AUTHOR

SIRONA KNIGHT is the author of many popular books on Wicca and Celtic spirituality, including *The Witch and Wizard Training Guide; The Wiccan Web; Celtic Traditions;* and *Love, Sex, and Magic.* A high priestess of the Celtic Gwyddonic Druid tradition, she holds a master's degree in psychology and is also a certified hypnotherapist. She lives in Northern California.

To purchase additional quality materials such as those included with this kit, please contact:

Aromaland, Inc.
1326 Rufina Circle
Santa Fe, NM 87505

800-933-5267

A wide variety of essential oils, aromatherapy blends, and accessories. Aromatherapy information and secure online shipping are available at their Web site: *www.buyaromatherapy.com*

The Crystal Courier
5974 N. Broadway
Denver, CO 80216

303-296-2820

Unique gift items from around the world, with an emphasis on New Age arts and crafts.

Spirit Dancer Sage
P.O. Box 644
Sedona, AZ 86339

928-282-7536

A fine selection of sacred herbs, smudging supplies, and ceremonial tools.